★ ★ ★ # KID ★ ★ ★
# ARTISTS
## TRUE TALES OF CHILDHOOD FROM
★ CREATIVE LEGENDS ★

STORIES BY *DAVID STABLER*   ILLUSTRATIONS BY *DOOGIE HORNER*

Library of Congress Cataloging in Publication Number: 2015956965

ISBN: 978-1-59474-896-7

Printed in China
Typeset in Bell, Bulmer, Avant Garde

Designed by Andie Reid based on a design by Doogie Horner
Illustrations by Doogie Horner
Illustration coloring by Mario Zucca
Production management by John J. McGurk

Quirk Books
215 Church Street
Philadelphia, PA 19106
quirkbooks.com

10 9 8 7 6 5 4 3 2 1

FRIDA KAHLO

LEONARDO DA VINCI

CHARLES SCHULZ

JEAN-MICHEL BASQUIAT

# ★ ★ ★ KID ★ ★ ★
# ARTISTS

## TRUE TALES OF CHILDHOOD FROM
## CREATIVE LEGENDS

STORIES BY *DAVID STABLER*  ILLUSTRATIONS BY *DOOGIE HORNER*

ANDY WARHOL

GEORGIA O'KEEFFE

PABLO PICASSO

BEATRIX POTTER

# TABLE OF CONTENTS

## PART THREE

## PRACTICE MAKES PERFECT

# INTRODUCTION

**N**ot every kid grows up to be a great artist. But every great artist *definitely* starts out as a kid. Painters get their start by doodling in school notebooks. Sculptors begin by playing with mud in their backyards. And most illustrators working today can name their favorite comic book, video game, or animated cartoon.

This book tells stories from the lives of sixteen legendary artists. You will surely recognize some of the names, but you've probably never heard such curious details about the artists' lives. That's because these stories take place *before* these painters, sculptors, and illustrators were famous—back when they were still kids doing homework, drawing in sketchpads, and dealing with moms and dads, brothers and sisters.

It's okay if you are not familiar with all the names in this book. You don't need to be. It's not necessary to see Andy Warhol's artworks to understand how much he did not want to go to school. He disliked school so much that, every morning, a grown-up had to drag him kicking and screaming out of the house.

On the other hand, you're probably quite familiar with the work of Dr. Seuss. Even so, you might not know that, as a kid, he was teased and bullied by his classmates. This book tells you why.

Then there's Jean-Michel Basquiat. His family had very little money, so he had to sleep in a crawlspace under the stairs.

And who could forget Charles Schulz? He entertained millions with comics about Charlie Brown and Snoopy. But did you know that his first published comic was about his family's real-life dog?

Each of the artists in this book had a special talent. Many of them also faced special challenges. Whether it was recovering from illness and injuries, like Frida Kahlo . . .

or dealing with an overprotective mother, like Yoko Ono . . .

or surviving a gruesome childhood accident, like
Jackson Pollock . . .

These kid artists all learned how great they could be
by surmounting huge obstacles. Or in the case of the
painter Emily Carr, just by rolling around in the mud
with some pigs!

We hope that this book will inspire you to draw, paint, and write stories of your very own. Maybe one day, you, too, will find your work hanging in a museum or published in the pages of a book! But even if that doesn't happen, we know you'll have a lot of fun just being creative and testing the limits of your imagination.

That's how all of these kid artists got started. They made art, they made a difference, and they made history.

# PART

# ONE

## CALL OF
## THE WILD

SECRET CAVES,
**CREEPY-CRAWLIES,**
AND **ANIMALS**
GALORE.

— THESE —

**KID ARTISTS**

WERE INSPIRED
AGAIN AND AGAIN
BY THE GREAT
OUTDOORS!

# LEONARDO DA VINCI

The Marvelous
Medusa Shield

He's best known for painting the *Mona Lisa*, a portrait of a woman with a mysterious and beguiling smile. But the Italian Renaissance artist Leonardo da Vinci's lost masterpiece was a terrifying vision straight out of a book of mythological monsters.

Nature always fascinated Leonardo da Vinci, who would grow up to be not only a great artist but also one of the Renaissance world's eminent scientists. Much of what he knew about animal and plant life he learned by taking long, solitary walks through the rolling hills of his native Tuscany, carrying a sketchbook in his hand. "While you are alone, you are completely yourself," he once said. "You should say to yourself, 'I will go my own way and withdraw apart from others, the better to study the form of natural objects.'"

But as fascinating as it was, the natural world could also be a source of great mystery and terror. Young Leonardo learned that lesson one day when he was walking alone in the countryside, hoping to see the "multitude of varied and strange forms created by nature."

He stumbled upon the entrance to a large cavern, deeper and darker than any he had ever seen. Leonardo lingered by the entrance to the cave for a long time. He bent down, peering into it, looking for signs of movement. He was afraid, but also intensely curious. Did he discern a monster lurking inside?

Leonardo never found out; he was too scared to explore any farther. But the vision of the cave creature stayed with him for the rest of his life, fueling his desire to depict the marvels of the natural world—and on one memorable occasion, the unnatural world as well.

In 1466, when Leonardo was fourteen years old, his father sent him to Florence to work as an apprentice to a renowned painter, sculptor, and goldsmith named Andrea del Verrocchio. Life in Verrocchio's workshop was often tedious. Leonardo spent his days grinding pigments, shopping for groceries, and running errands for the master. He worked hard and was rewarded with invaluable instruction in the arts of drawing, painting, and anatomy. Leonardo quickly became one of Verrocchio's prize pupils and grew into a formidable artist in his own right.

One day, according to a sixteenth-century art historian named Giorgio Vasari, a farmer friend presented Leonardo's father, Ser Piero da Vinci, with a round shield made of fig wood; he asked to have it decorated in Florence. Leonardo's father passed the job on to his son, instructing Leonardo to paint an image on the front of the shield.

In his quest for inspiration, Leonardo thought long and hard, wracking his brain for a suitably terrifying subject to adorn a warrior's shield. What could he paint that would be so horrible that it would frighten anyone who gazed upon it? Perhaps it was then that Leonardo thought back to his past experience of peering into the darkened cave in search of a monster.

All of a sudden the idea came to him. Leonardo remembered the Greek legend of Medusa, a monstrous Gorgon whose hair was made of poisonous snakes.

It was said that anyone who looked upon her face would instantly be turned to stone. What better way to vanquish your opponent than by petrifying him with Medusa's glowering head on your shield?

And so that's what Leonardo painted. He retreated to his room in Verrocchio's workshop, directing all the power of his imagination into creating a hideous image of the serpent-haired Medusa leaping out from behind a mound of broken stones, spitting venom, breathing fire, and sending smoke pouring out of her nostrils. It was a horrible sight to behold—and Leonardo loved it.

When the shield was finished, Leonardo summoned his father to pick it up. Ser Piero arrived in the early morning, eager to return the commission to the farmer and collect payment. He knocked on his son's door, but Leonardo cracked it only a little and told him to wait a moment. He then went back and into his room and shuttered the window, creating total darkness, with only a single shaft of light illuminating the shield. Then Leonardo beckoned his father to enter.

As soon as he saw the shield, Ser Piero staggered backward. Convinced that a gargoyle or some other awful monstrosity had perched itself on the shield, he turned to run away. But Leonardo stopped him. "The work answers the purpose for which it was made," he declared. "That was the effect I wanted to produce!"

Ser Piero refused the shield. He could not bear the thought of subjecting anyone else to the same macabre surprise he had just experienced. Instead, he found another shield, painted it with the image of a heart pierced by a dart, and gave it to his farmer friend.

So what ever happened to Leonardo's Medusa? According to legend, Ser Piero sold the shield to a group of Florentine merchants for a hundred ducats. They in turn sold the artwork to the Duke of Milan for three times that price. But no one is really sure. The shield has long since vanished, a lost treasure from the old master's childhood that continues to haunt us. Who knows? Perhaps one day someone will discover the horrifying shield, buried among the treasures in a dusty antiques store.

# VINCENT VAN GOGH

The Boy Who Loved Bugs

**H**e would grow up to become one of the most illustrious artists in the world, known for his swirling images of people, plants, and the night skies. But to his neighbors back in the Netherlands, Vincent van Gogh was just a peculiar and fiercely determined kid who loved to collect insects.

Every day, neighbors would watch Vincent van
Gogh walk down the hill. Through the garden gate
he'd go, out into the fields behind his house in search of
the elusive water beetles that fascinated him. He carried
a glass jar and an old fishing net—the better to skim
the beasties off the surface of the creek.

Vincent spent hours sitting on the banks of the
stream, waiting silently for a shiny black critter to
appear. Each one was unique. Some had crooked legs
that wriggled when you plucked them out of the water.
Others had long, fearsome-looking antennae.

Vincent knew the names of all the different types
of bugs. When he caught one, he'd drop it in his jar for
safekeeping during the long trek back home. There, in
his attic bedroom, he delivered the bugs to their final
resting place. He took great care pinning the collected

beetles inside tiny specimen boxes. Onto each box he glued a label with the Latin name of its dearly departed inhabitant. Sometimes he would show the bugs to his sisters before he boxed them up. The girls were horrified.

FRANK    HANS    WOLFGANG

But Vincent didn't care what anyone thought about his hobbies. He loved nature, collecting things, and being by himself. On summer days, he'd gather handfuls of wildflowers from the meadow; it was said that he had memorized the spots where only the rarest flowers bloomed.

Other times he spent hours staring at birds, studying their movements. He became an expert on avian migration. When the birds flew south for the winter, he set out to find their nests and then added them to his nature collection.

Vincent's mother shared his love of the outdoors, but she worried that he was spending too much time alone in the fields. She tried to convince him to pick up a hobby, like drawing. She gave him art books, pencils, and sketchpads and encouraged him to trace the images he saw in the paintings.

But Vincent quickly grew bored with copying, and once again he ventured into the meadow to sketch his own vision of nature. He wasn't happy with his drawings, however, and rarely showed them to anyone. He later called them nothing more than "little scratches."

Only one person could get Vincent to change his solitary ways: his younger brother Theo. Theo was Vincent's opposite in every way. Cheerful, friendly, and fun-loving, Theo loved spending time with people. He had none of Vincent's gloomy disposition and shared none of his eccentricities. While Vincent liked to study birds and collect their nests, Theo preferred to whistle along with their songs.

For a time, Theo's sunny personality rubbed off on Vincent. Though they were four years apart in age, they became roommates, playmates, and constant companions. Vincent taught Theo how to shoot marbles and invented elaborate games to play. In summer, they built sandcastles in the family garden. When winter came, they skated on the pond or dragged their sleds through the snow. If it was too cold to go outside, they stayed indoors and played board games by the fireside.

But Vincent soon fell into a sad funk. It didn't help that he felt as if Theo was their parents' favorite. The kids in town also took an immediate liking to Theo, which only worsened the sibling rivalry.

Vincent grew ever more resentful. Once the closest of friends, the brothers began arguing more frequently. Overcome with sadness, Vincent withdrew and once again sought solace in nature. When he passed Theo on his way to the creek to collect bugs, he ignored him.

Vincent's behavior—and his appearance—grew increasingly bizarre. He trudged through town with his head down, glowering at neighbors from behind the brim of a straw hat, wandering off the beaten paths into the wild countryside on long walkabouts.

To his parents' dismay, Vincent loved to venture out at night, especially when a storm was brewing. He once disappeared for several hours, ending up in a town six miles away. When he returned home in the middle of the night, his clothes were filthy and his shoes were caked in mud.

At home, Vincent became quarrelsome and prone to tantrums. The family maid complained that he was the most unpleasant of all the Van Gogh children. She branded him an *oarige*, the Dutch word for "oddball."

At first, even art brought no satisfaction to Vincent, and his temper could be destructive. He once drew a picture of a cat climbing an apple tree. But when he showed it to his mother, she failed to give him the approval he was seeking. Vincent tore up the sketch. When he was eight years old, a sculptor's assistant gave him some clay, which he expertly molded into an elephant. But Vincent was so dissatisfied with his sculpture that he smashed it on the floor.

OH MAN. I DIDN'T LOOK THAT BAD.

Shortly after turning sixteen, Vincent got a job in an art gallery in the Hague. He spent the next four years packing and unpacking art supplies, boxing up paintings, and getting an up-close look at the works of the great Dutch masters, including Rembrandt van Rijn and Jan Vermeer.

Being left alone seemed to revive Vincent's spirits. He handled the artworks as carefully as he had once collected the insects, becoming as devoted to the study of art as he was to the world of nature. He even made up with Theo, who visited him in the Hague and later followed him into the art business. The brothers began writing long letters to each other in which Vincent confessed his feelings of loneliness and isolation and his desire to express himself through his art.

It would be another decade before Vincent was able to dedicate himself full-time to painting. In the meantime, he endured many personal and professional setbacks. Over the years, he poured all his unhappiness and his energy into making art. Although he was never able to recapture the serenity he had found as a child skimming water bugs off the stream near his house, he did manage to convey the intensity of his feelings about nature—and his own personality—in many of his paintings.

Theo remained one of the few bright spots in Vincent's life. Besides exchanging regular letters— more than six hundred in all—Theo also sent Vincent money and introduced his brother to many of the important artists of the day, including Paul Gauguin and Paul Cézanne. Until the end, Theo served as his older brother's bridge to the outside world—and the best friend this lonely artist ever had.

# BEATRIX POTTER

Nature
Girl

S he may have been born in the city, but Beatrix Potter was a country girl at heart. The author of such classic illustrated books as *The Tale of Peter Rabbit* found her first artistic inspiration on a sprawling estate in the Scottish countryside. There she discovered the love of animals and of drawing that would make her one of the world's most beloved storytellers.

The first time she saw her family's new vacation house, Beatrix Potter knew it was the place for her. "Home sweet home," she called it. The local name for the house was Dalguise. Beatrix was just five years old when her parents decided to rent the country estate, which lay nestled in the woods along the River Tay, in the heart of the Scottish Highlands. It became her summertime refuge for the next eleven years.

Dalguise was nothing like the Potters' house back in London, a dark and drafty mansion known as Bolton Gardens. After being cooped up all year in the big city, catered to by servants and mostly ignored by her rich parents, Beatrix looked forward to the annual excursion to the north country. The lush green fields of Scotland were like an exciting new world, teeming with strange plants and interesting wildlife. The sights and smells of the nearby cottages and farms never ceased to enchant her. At first she explored by herself. Then, when her younger brother Bertram grew old enough, she had a playmate to go on adventures with.

Although Beatrix was rich in material things—thanks to her wealthy parents—she lacked true friendship. Her mother would not let her play with other children for fear she would catch germs, so Bertram became Beatrix's constant companion. Though they were five years apart in age, they shared a curiosity about the natural world. Together they would wander through the woods and along the stony beaches of the River Tay, scooping up plants, animals, and insects for their collection of nature specimens.

Beatrix and Bertram had many adventures at Dalguise. One day they found a dead fox in the woods.

They took it back to the house, skinned it, and boiled it until there was nothing left but bones, which they then proceeded to reconstruct into a skeleton.

The two also created specimen books, filling the pages with drawings of birds' eggs, butterflies, and flowers. Beatrix discovered she was good at making these detailed illustrations, and soon she branched out into recording larger animals and plants. The children even unearthed an old printing press and started stamping out woodcuts of nature scenes, using a homemade ink they concocted by themselves.

When the summer ended, Beatrix and Bertram returned to London, where they continued their studies of the specimens they smuggled home from Dalguise. The family butler, Cox, was enlisted to sneak small animals up to the third-floor bedroom the children shared. In time, they amassed a small menagerie that included several mice, assorted rabbits, a hedgehog and some bats, a family of snails, a frog named Punch, a pair of lizards named Toby and Judy, and a fourteen-inch-long ring snake they called Sally.

Whenever Beatrix wanted to draw the animals, her brother would let them out of their cages so they could "pose" for her. The hedgehog, in particular, did not seem to like sitting for portraits. "So long as she can go to sleep on my knee she is delighted," Beatrix reported. "But if she is propped up on end for half an hour, she first begins to yawn . . . and then she does bite!"

Some of Beatrix's drawings were realistic. Others were more fanciful. She drew rabbits that walked upright on two legs, wore bonnets, carried umbrellas, or ice-skated. More and more, she started dreaming up stories about the animals in the natural world.

When Beatrix was ten years old, Bertram left home to attend boarding school. Beatrix was sorry to lose her trusted friend but determined to continue with her drawing. In those days, girls did not go to school, so Beatrix was educated at home by a series of private teachers, called governesses. One governess, Miss Hammond, presented Beatrix with a paint box so she could add color to her illustrations. On weekends, Miss Hammond took Beatrix to the Kensington Natural History Museum. Beatrix spent the entire morning sketching the animals in their display cases.

Over the next few years, Beatrix made hundreds of natural history sketches, including several dozen drawings of mushrooms. But with her brother away at school, she didn't have a way to share her experiences with others. Then one summer, while on vacation with her parents, she met Canon Hardwicke Rawnsley, a young priest. He took an immediate interest in Beatrix's artwork and encouraged her to start recording her impressions in a diary.

At first Beatrix was skeptical. She was good at drawing, but writing? That was something entirely different. "What would I put in a diary?" she asked. "I don't do anything exciting."

"Why, everything that happens," Canon Rawnsley replied. "The places you visit, people you talk to, stories you hear. It isn't so much what you write—it's doing it regularly that counts. And the more you write, the easier you'll find it. Do try it!"

Beatrix decided to accept Rawnsley's challenge. But first she took steps to ensure that no one could read her diary without permission. She composed her entries in a secret code that only she could decipher. She also wrote in a tiny cramped script that would strain prying eyes.

Just as Rawnsley had predicted, the diary turned out to be a great way for Beatrix to express herself. She ended up keeping a journal for more than sixteen years. It became the place where she recorded sketches, jokes and stories from the newspaper, comments on the plants and animals she encountered, and descriptions of nature scenes that would later become the settings for some of her classic children's stories.

As Beatrix grew older, she became less shy about sharing her stories with others. Whenever she went away on vacation, she sent letters to the children of her friends and former governesses. Over the course of her life, she wrote more than a thousand such letters, often accompanied by sketches of small animals like those she had encountered at Dalguise. One of these "picture letters" became the basis of her first book, *The Tale of Peter Rabbit,* published in 1902. Today it is considered one of the most popular children's books of all time.

Beatrix would remain deeply interested in the natural world for the rest of her life. She contributed detailed illustrations of mushrooms and fungus spores to leading scientific organizations. She also began farming and raising sheep, and she soon had a flock that numbered in the thousands. In fact, Beatrix was so successful that she became the first woman elected president of the Herdwick Sheepherders' Association.

But despite these achievements, Beatrix is best remembered for her children's books, which have sold millions of copies worldwide. Many of the characters she invented were inspired by real people and animals she encountered as a child. The title character in her 1905 book *The Tale of Mrs. Tiggy Winkle,* for example, was a combination of her pet hedgehog—the one that disliked posing for pictures—and a Scottish washerwoman named Kitty MacDonald.

In all, Beatrix would publish twenty-three tales for kids. Today, more than a century later, Beatrix Potter fans from all over the world still flock to the house in the highlands where so many of her stories began.

# EMILY CARR

*Out of the Woods*

oday she is one of Canada's best-known artists, celebrated for her love of animals and the great outdoors. But Emily Carr was raised to be a prim-and-proper English girl. To find her true calling, she had to break with the old traditions and venture deep into the heart of the British Columbia wilderness.

Emily Carr was what is called a late bloomer. It took her a long time to achieve recognition as an artist. But when she finally did, she took to the creative life with great gusto.

Growing up in western Canada, Emily became known for her eccentric behavior. She was easy to spot in a crowd. That's because wherever she went, a troop of animals traveled with her—and not just cats and dogs but parrots, chipmunks, white rats, and a raccoon. One of her pets became something of a local celebrity. It was a Javanese monkey whom she named Woo, after the noise it made. As an adult, Emily was known to wheel Woo around in an old baby carriage.

Emily's three older sisters didn't approve of Woo, or of her unconventional ways, but that didn't bother

Emily. She never let the opinions of other people stop her from being true to herself.

Emily may have been a rebel at heart, but her staid upbringing was that of a well-mannered British schoolgirl. Her father, Richard Carr, was born in England and remained proud of his heritage. He chose to settle his family on Canada's Vancouver Island, a colony of Great Britain, so they could continue to practice the English customs he loved so much.

The second youngest of nine children, Emily grew up in a stately mansion, complete with an English garden. The house was a five-hour ferry ride to the Canadian mainland, so the Carrs may as well have been living in the center of London for all Emily knew. Because their mother was in poor health, the children's day-to-day needs were tended to by servants, including an Indian washerwoman named Mary and a Chinese cook named Bong.

YOUR BANANA SPLIT SUNDAE, MY LADY.

THANK YOU KINDLY.

Richard Carr was a successful grocer who ran the household with military precision. "When father commanded, everybody ran," Emily later recalled. He had all sorts of rules to be obeyed, especially at mealtimes. For dinner, Mr. Carr forbade Bong from serving a roast that weighed less than ten pounds. At breakfast, he insisted that the children's bread be topped with butter or jam, but not both. Only on Sundays did he allow them to sample the two spreads together.

Emily's older sister Edith acted as the enforcer of household edicts. Every evening at exactly six o'clock, she ordered Emily to collect all her toys, put away her dolls, wash her face, and put on clean clothes in time for their father's arrival home from work. If any friends from the neighborhood were in the house, they quickly scurried for the door.

At first, Emily didn't question her father's rules. As she grew older, however, she began to rebel against the limitations he placed on her. She also resented Edith's zeal in meting out punishment for disobedience.

With her father often away on business trips and her mother confined to a sickbed, Emily sought refuge in the two things she loved best: art and nature. She had learned to draw at an early age. When she was eight years old, she completed her first successful sketch: a portrait of the family dog.

"I sat beside Carlow's kennel and stared at him for a long time," she later remembered. "Then I took a charred stick from the grate, split open a large brown-paper sack, and drew a dog on the sack."

HOW ABOUT THIS POSE?
SORT OF A GREEK THING?

HMMM...

Emily's strait-laced father recognized her artistic ability and encouraged her to pursue it. He built an easel out of branches from an old cherry tree and paid for her art lessons so she could develop her skills. But he began to have second thoughts when Emily got in trouble at school for drawing faces on her fingernails, among other transgressions.

Always a mischievous child, Emily loved to play outdoors, and she loved animals, too. Her family kept a barnyard full of cows and pigs, and she liked nothing better than to roll around in the mud with them. Sometimes she wore her best dresses on these mucky romps.

Other times she dressed starfish and myriad little creatures in doll's clothes, just to see the look on her siblings' faces.

Behind the Carr family's house was an acre of forest populated by hooting owls and croaking frogs. Emily loved to go exploring in the woods. She would pick up wild animals and bring them home. Her adopted family included ducks, chickens, and a baby crow.

Beyond the forest lay the center of town, where Emily liked to sit on warm summer days and watch people pass by. Once she saw a group of prisoners heading to the city jail. All the men were dressed in an identical outfit of checkered shirt, moleskin trousers, and blue cloth cap. Emily brought her sketchbook along so she could record such unusual sights.

When Emily was fourteen years old, her life took a turn for the worse: her mother died of tuberculosis. Two years later, beset by grief, her father also passed away. Emily's sister Edith now became the head of the household. Unfortunately, Edith was just as stern as their father had been, and twice as harsh. She increasingly resorted to spanking to keep Emily from misbehaving.

After one such punishment, Emily decided enough was enough. "I am almost sixteen now, and the next time you thrash me I shall strike back!" she told Edith. That was the last time her sister dared to strike her.

Fortunately, Emily could find some comfort with the animals she loved. The next time she felt like heading out into the woods, she mounted her horse Johnny. Johnny was a former circus pony who knew the local countryside almost as well as she did.

Emily thought she was just going for their usual canter through the forest, but the horse had other ideas. This time Johnny set off on a gallop through the woods.

WHOOOAH!

He rode past the town and over the roadway until they had ventured into unknown territory. Then he slowed his pace, stopping now and again to sniff the bushes along the roadside.

When he determined that the path was safe, Johnny pushed forward into the underbrush, forging trails through the greenery. The bushes closed up behind them, leaving horse and rider truly alone, hidden from the town and all its inhabitants.

Eventually Johnny carried Emily to a moss-covered clearing. There he stopped and let out a great sigh that told Emily they had arrived. Gently, she released the bridle and let him nibble on the grass. At that moment, as she beheld the deep woods she had never visited before, Emily realized that her place was not back in the house, with her sisters' rules and punishments, but out in the great Canadian wilderness with the animals she loved so much.

Emily would visit the clearing with Johnny many times. Eventually, she left Canada to study art in the

United States and Europe. But she returned later in life, and she spent many years celebrating the country's natural beauty in her sketches and paintings.

After Emily Carr became a painter, she wrote about her decision to leave home. She told the story of rides into the woods with Johnny, and she thanked her pony for helping her discover "the deep lovely places that were the very foundation on which my work as a painter was to be built."

# GEORGIA O'KEEFFE

Born a
Rebel

**K**nown for her nearly abstract paintings of flowers, animal skulls, and desert landscapes, Georgia O'Keeffe had a unique way of looking at the world. In fact, everything about her was completely original. From the way she dressed to the way she painted, she made it cool to be unconventional.

"From the time I was small," Georgia O'Keeffe once said, "I was always doing things people don't do." Indeed, as a little girl, Georgia prided herself on being different from other kids. "If my sisters wore their hair braided, I wouldn't wear mine braided," she recalled. "If they wore ribbons, I wouldn't."

Georgia was always challenging her sisters to be bolder and braver. The dairy farm where they lived in rural Wisconsin offered plenty of opportunities for mischief. One time, Georgia snuck her sisters into the barnyard, a place the girls were not allowed to go. They tiptoed inside the cow pen, where she dared them to stick their hands inside a cow's mouth to feel the tongue. Naturally, Georgia had no fear of doing so herself. Years later, "Licking Cow" became the subject of one of her paintings.

This rebellious streak put Georgia on a collision course with her stern Aunt Jennie, who enforced all the rules in the O'Keeffe household. Aunt Jennie was constantly punishing Georgia for misbehaving. It's no wonder that Georgia once called her "the headache of my life."

To make matters worse, Aunt Jennie was constantly praising Georgia's older brother Francis. So Georgia decided to be better than Francis at everything. She outstudied, outraced, and outclimbed him every chance she got. But no one in her family ever noticed.

Georgia soon learned that being the black sheep in the family had its advantages. With Francis getting so much attention from the grown-ups, Georgia was free to sneak off and explore outdoors. She'd spend hours sitting under the apple trees on her farm, or gazing up at the clouds, or carefully examining the petals of brightly colored wildflowers. One time she even ate dirt just to find out what it tasted like.

Georgia loved nature, but at first she had no way to express how the natural world made her feel—until she learned to draw. That happened when she was nine years old and she began attending art classes.

In those days, young girls were usually sent to study art so they could learn how to decorate their homes when they got married. Of course, Georgia had other ideas. She wanted to make art for herself, not for some future husband.

Georgia spent hours studying the fundamentals of drawing, endlessly copying cubes, squares, and spheres out of an art instruction book. By practicing drawing geometric shapes, Georgia became so good at drawing that even her mother took notice. At last, she was better at something than Francis!

MOVE OVER REMBRANDT!

Georgia's mother decided to send her daughter for private lessons given by a local painter named Sarah Mann. Every Saturday, Georgia made the seven-mile round-trip buggy ride to Ms. Mann's home in Sun Prairie. In these classes, Georgia was not asked to copy whatever images were put in front of her. Instead, she was allowed to choose what she wanted to draw. Some of Georgia's early works included an Arabian horse and a single red rose.

By age twelve, Georgia knew she wanted to be an artist. "I decided that the only thing I could do that was nobody else's business was to paint," she once said. "I could do as I chose because no one would care." But her need for complete freedom would be tested at the next stop on her journey: the Sacred Heart Convent School in Madison, Wisconsin.

Georgia enrolled at Sacred Heart at age fourteen, and the rules were stricter than anything she had ever experienced. The nuns who ran the school controlled every aspect of the students' lives. Each girl was required to wear a black veil to attend chapel every morning, and they all had to wear black on Sundays. The nuns could stop any student at any time to inspect her mail or read what she was writing in her notebook.

WE'RE KEEPING OUR EYES ON YOU, YOUNG LADY!

On Georgia's first day in the school's art studio, an instructor named Sister Angelique handed her a lump of charcoal and told her to draw a baby's hand. Georgia did the best she could, but her teacher did not approve of the results.

Other kids might have given up, but Georgia saw the criticism as a challenge. She decided to do everything she could to meet—and exceed—Sister Angelique's tough standards. Her drawings became larger and larger.

At the end of the school year, Georgia won two medals: one for "for improvement in illustration and drawing" and the other for deportment, or good behavior. It was Georgia's first good-conduct prize—and it would be her last. She would soon return to her rebellious ways.

The next year, Georgia and her family moved from Wisconsin to Williamsburg, Virginia. She enrolled at Chatham Episcopal Institute, an expensive boarding

school that was very different from Sacred Heart. At
Chatham, the teachers gave Georgia total freedom,
although the other students had trouble accepting her
unconventional behavior. Some girls made fun of her
Wisconsin accent and unusual clothes. Most of the girls
wore ruffled dresses and put elaborate ribbons in their
hair, but Georgia preferred drab, loose-fitting coats. She
twisted her hair into one long braid that ran halfway
down her back. Her appearance was unusual compared
to that of her classmates, but Georgia didn't mind being
different.

Fortunately, there was a bright spot at school.
Georgia's art teacher, Elizabeth Willis, recognized her
new student's ability almost immediately. She provided
Georgia with her own table in a private studio and

allowed her to work at her own pace. When the other students complained that Georgia was being given special treatment, Mrs. Willis defended her decision: "When the spirit moves Georgia, she can do more in a day than you can do in a week."

Mrs. Willis taught Georgia to look at the natural world in exciting and unusual ways. She encouraged Georgia to hold wildflowers and examine the blooms from different angles. Then Georgia would try drawing the same flower over and over, sometimes showing only parts of the blossom or simplifying the shapes until they were barely recognizable. It was a technique she would use later in the more than two hundred flower paintings she produced during her career as an artist.

Outside the classroom, Georgia was constantly playing practical jokes and drawing caricatures of her teachers. Her penchant for defying authority started to win over the other students. She stayed out after curfew, teaching the other girls card games like poker.

With acceptance and popularity came opportunities. Soon Georgia was named art editor of the school yearbook. When she graduated from Chatham in June 1905, Georgia's classmates wrote a poem about her and had it printed under her yearbook photo:

*A girl who would be different in habit, style, and dress.*
*A girl who doesn't give a cent for men—and boys still less.*
*O is for O'Keeffe; an artist divine.*
*Her paintings are perfect and her drawings are fine.*

Georgia O'Keeffe went on to enjoy a long career as an artist, passing away in 1987, at the age of ninety-eight. She continued working right up until the end of her life and never compromised on her artistic vision. Though Georgia gave many interviews over the years, and was asked many times to describe her special way of looking at the world, she preferred to let her work speak for itself. As she once explained: "I found I could say things with color and shapes that I couldn't say any other way—things I had no words for."

# TWO

## IT'S A HARD-KNOCK LIFE

SHYNESS, POVERTY, **DISCRIMINATION,** AND WAR. BEFORE THEY HIT THE **BIG TIME,** ——— THESE ———

## KID ARTISTS

OVERCAME **ALL KINDS OF** OBSTACLES.

# LOUISE NEVELSON

Coming to America

What's it like to leave your home and move to a country where you don't know anybody and can't speak the language? As a young immigrant freshly arrived in the United States, Louise Nevelson was the ultimate new kid in school. The streets of this foreign land may not have been paved with gold, but sometimes the hardest road leads to the greatest reward.

In the spring of 1905, a five-year-old girl named Leah Berliawsky boarded a steamship bound for Boston. Traveling with her were her mother Minna, her older brother Nachman, and her baby sister Chaya. The close-knit Russian Jewish family was on their way across the Atlantic Ocean to America to reunite with Leah's father, Isaac. It was the last leg of a three-month journey—and the first step in Leah's transformation into Louise Nevelson, one of the most celebrated sculptors of the twentieth century.

Leah's new home would be different from the one she left behind. In Russia, Leah was raised in a shtetl, a small town where Jewish families lived according to traditional customs. Her earliest memories were of marketplaces teeming with peasant women and peddlers haggling in a centuries-old language called Yiddish.

The shtetl was a happy environment for Leah. But Russia at that time could also be a dangerous place for Jewish people, who often faced discrimination because of their religion.

When Leah was three years old, her father decided to seek a fresh start in the United States. He promised to send for his family once he got established. Leah was so her upset at her father's departure that she stopped talking for six months. At first, her mother was afraid she'd been struck deaf or mute. But Leah was just quietly protesting the separation of her family.

LEAH, TALK TO ME! WHAT'S WRONG?

Leah used this time of silence to develop her powers of observation. Because she wouldn't ask for anything, she had to learn by watching others. She became more aware of colors, gazing with rapt attention as her grandmother soaked wool clothing in brightly colored vegetable dyes to turn them different shades.

By 1905, Isaac Berliawsky had finally saved up
enough money to pay for his family's passage to his
new home in America. Minna and the children loaded
all their belongings into a wagon for the start of the
voyage. After traveling overland to the German city of
Hamburg, they boarded a cramped ocean liner crowded
with hundreds of other immigrants just like them.

The lower deck of the boat was more unpleasant
than Leah could have imagined. People huddled
together for warmth, or they jostled for a share of the
paltry helpings of soup being ladled out by the ship's
cooks. Foul smells lingered in the air as bouts of sea-
sickness rolled through the passengers on board. When
an outbreak of measles struck, Leah's family was forced
to spend six weeks under quarantine in Liverpool,
England. That turned out to be a lucky break. It was

there that Leah made two discoveries that impressed her forever.

Because she spoke no English, Leah communicated through her eyes, not her mouth. On one of her strolls around Liverpool, she visited a candy shop for the first time. Row after row of glass jars, each filled with a different-colored hard candy, glimmered under the bright lights inside the shop. After spending so much time in the dark, dank hold of a steamship, Leah felt as if she were seeing a rainbow.

Leah's second important discovery happened when she was playing with some girls. Leah watched in amazement as one of the girls picked up a doll and its eyes opened, then closed again when it was set down. Leah had never seen anything like it back in Russia.

Surely the doll must be magic, she thought. Would her new home on the other side of the ocean be filled with wonders such as this?

Once the quarantine was lifted, Leah and her family were allowed to board the ship and proceed to Boston. They were met there by a Russian-born relative named Joseph Dondis. He explained to Leah's mother that the children should change their names to better fit in among Americans. Leah became Louise, Nachman became Nathan, and Chaya became Annie. Joseph then secured them passage on yet another boat that would reunite them with Isaac in the city where he had settled: Rockland, Maine.

The next day, the Berliawskys arrived in their new hometown. Isaac met them at the wharf and brought them to the rooming house where they would live for the next several years. But if Louise thought the hard times were over now that she had arrived in America, she was wrong. Just as on the ship, the Berliawskys found themselves fighting for space. The rooming house was teeming with fellow immigrants.

Not only that, but discrimination had not been left behind, either. Louise soon discovered that hers was one of only a handful of Jewish families in town. Although they were treated better than they had been in Russia, Louise still felt like an outsider.

At school, Louise struggled with English. Kids teased her for speaking Yiddish and for the flamboyant clothes her mother bought for her. Fancy dresses and feathered hats were considered signs of sophistication back in Russia. But in Maine, where people dressed more plainly, they were thought of as strange.

School offered one bright spot, however. Louise loved her art class. From the moment she arrived in America, Louise spent all her free time drawing. It was her way of escaping from the unfamiliar world in which she found herself, and it allowed her to express her feelings without using words. One day, her teacher brought in colored chalk. Like the rainbow candies she had seen in the sweets shop in Liverpool, the chalk seemed to stir something inside her.

Another time, when Louise was in second grade, her teacher showed a picture of a sunflower and asked the class to draw it from memory. While the other students tried to reproduce the image exactly, Louise drew the sunflower as she saw it in her mind's eye: a large brown circle surrounded by tiny yellow petals. The teacher held up Louise's imaginative drawing for special praise, declaring it the most original interpretation in the class. It was the first time Louise had been singled out for something positive.

After that, Louise began studying with a drawing teacher named Lena Cleveland. At first, Miss Cleveland thought Louise was copying her drawings out of a book. But soon she realized Louise was working hard to improve her skills. Louise also liked that Miss Cleveland came to class wearing a bright purple coat and hat. Maybe, Louise thought, her own style of dress wasn't so odd after all.

Slowly, Louise began to feel more comfortable in her adopted country. With new-found confidence, she started to think about pursuing a career in art. It took a chance encounter with a great medieval heroine to help her decide what type of artist she wanted to be.

That encounter took place one day when she was nine years old. Louise went to the Rockland Public Library, where she saw a sculpture of Joan of Arc made entirely of plaster. Like many old statues, this one was covered in a thin greenish layer called a patina. The figure had an otherworldly glow that left a powerful impression in Louise's imagination.

As Louise was leaving, the librarian asked what she wanted to be when she grew up. "An artist!" Louise blurted out without even thinking. Then she paused and reconsidered. "I'm going to be a sculptor," she said. "I don't want color to help me."

And so it was decided. Louise Berliawsky—who would become Louise Nevelson after marrying Charles

Nevelson in 1920—grew up to become one of the most original American sculptors of the twentieth century. She worked almost exclusively in black and white, but when she added color to her sculptures, she did so with a purpose. Late in life, she completed a series of sculptures painted entirely in gold. It was her way of acknowledging her immigrant experience. When her family left Russia, Louise said, "They promised that the streets of America would be paved in gold."

Like many immigrants, Louise Nevelson discovered that the path to prosperity was a lot rougher than she had anticipated. But through tenacity, perseverance, and a dedication to her art, she forged a golden ending all her own.

I'VE COME A LONG WAY FROM THE SHTETL!

# DR. SEUSS

> ## And to Think That He Saw It on Mulberry Street

**T**here really is a Mulberry Street. It runs through Springfield, Massachusetts, the hometown of Ted Geisel—better known to the world as Dr. Seuss. It was in Springfield that Ted first began to write, draw, and rhyme in his distinctive style. It was also where he learned an important lesson about discrimination.

From the beginning, Ted Geisel loved two things more than all else: funny animals and silly words.

When Ted was a boy, he lived six blocks away from the town zoo. On summer days, when school was out, he'd head over to the zoo and spend hours gazing at the monkeys in their monkey house and the lions in their cages. Then he'd rush home and—with his parents' permission—draw pictures of the animals in crayon on his bedroom walls.

The surprising thing was that Ted's animals looked nothing like the real ones. The creatures resembled cartoons—a duck with angel wings for example. He would label each one with its own nonsensical name. One of his favorite imaginary beasts was an elephant with nine-foot-long ears, which he called a Wynnmph.

Ted's love of inventive words and funny sayings ran in the family. His grandfather had immigrated to America from Germany in the mid-1800s. Together with a man named Christian Kalmbach, he founded a brewery called Kalmbach and Geisel, which sounded a lot like "Come Back and Guzzle." So that's what people started calling it. By the time Ted was born, in 1904, his grandfather's brewery was one of the largest and most successful in New England. Its beer was delivered all over Springfield in a black and gold wagon pulled by Clydesdale horses.

Ted's father helped run the business, and in his spare time he invented things and gave them funny names. His inventions included a machine for strengthening the muscles in a person's forearm, and a device that prevented flies from getting into beer barrels. Ted's favorite was a mysterious contraption called the Silk-Stocking-Back-Seam-Wrong-Detecting Mirror.

Ted's older sister shared his love for weird and wacky words. Her name was Margaretha, but she insisted that everyone call her Marnie Mecca Ding Ding Guy. Nobody knows why.

Ted's mother's specialty was stringing words into a rhythm called a meter. Back when she was young, Henrietta Seuss Geisel had worked in her family's bakery. Later, after she married Ted's father, Henrietta would sing her infant son a lullaby about the pies she used to sell: "Apple, mince, lemon…peach, apricot, pineapple…blueberry, coconut, custard, and SQUASH!" The meter stuck in Ted's head, helping him remember all the different kinds of pies.

Besides his love of wordplay, Ted had yet another reason for being fascinated with language. He was bilingual, meaning that he spoke two languages, German and English. At Christmastime, the family sang "Stille Nacht" instead of "Silent Night" and "O Tannenbaum" instead of "O Christmas Tree." For dinner, Ted ate German sausages, and he learned to appreciate the many varieties of liverwurst.

BREZEL     BRATWURST     KARTOFFELPUFFER

SPÄTZLE     SPARGEL     APFELSTRUDEL

Ted never thought much about his German background, or how it made him different from other kids in Springfield. But that all changed when Ted turned thirteen. That year the United States went to war with Germany. A patriotic fervor took hold in America, and some people directed their anger toward the German Americans in their communities.

Families like the Geisels became objects of suspicion. People feared they might be spies or traitors secretly loyal to the German ruler, Kaiser Wilhelm. Some U.S. government officials encouraged such anti-German sentiment. A special committee of Congress officially renamed frankfurters "hot dogs," and sauerkraut became "liberty cabbage."

The wave of misplaced patriotism soon reached Springfield. Town leaders ordered that all German-language books be removed from the library. The local symphony stopped playing music by German composers. The pastor at the local Lutheran church started preaching in English instead of German. Some of Ted's classmates teased him for speaking German at home. They called him the "Kaiser's Kid" and threw stones at him.

Ted refused to be bullied. Over the next few months, he set out to prove that German Americans could be just as patriotic as anyone else—even more so. He collected scraps of tin for the war effort and planted a victory garden in his yard.

IT'S HARD WORK PULLING ALL OF THOSE WEEDS.

BUT A GARDEN IS SOMETHING THAT EVERYONE NEEDS!

When his Boy Scout troop asked members to sell war bonds, Ted was among the first to volunteer. For the next several weeks, he went door to door, up and down Mulberry Street, convincing the citizens of Springfield to buy bonds to support American soldiers fighting in the war. Ted even persuaded his own grandfather to pledge $1,000.

Ted was so successful that he was named one of Springfield's top ten Boy Scout war-bonds salesmen.

To honor the boys, a special ceremony was held in the town's auditorium. Presenting the awards was a very special master of ceremonies: former U.S. president Theodore Roosevelt.

On the day of the event, thousands of townspeople crowded the auditorium. Ted was on the stage, along with his scoutmaster and the nine other honorees. As patriotic music played, President Roosevelt approached the podium. He delivered a rousing welcome speech and then proceeded down the line to pin a medal on each boy's chest.

When he got to Ted, however, he had no more medals to pin! Ted stood there awkwardly. He was so embarrassed.

WHAT'S THIS
LITTLE BOY
DOING HERE?

As it turned out, Ted's scoutmaster had miscounted, giving the president only nine medals instead of ten. Ted had the misfortune of being last in line.

The scoutmaster hastily whisked Ted off the stage. Even though it was just bad luck, Ted felt like he was being punished for being German. The memory of this mortifying moment never faded. For the rest of his life, Ted feared appearing onstage in front of large crowds.

By the time the war ended, Ted was a sophomore in high school. Springfield's German American citizens went back to their normal lives; few spoke of the discrimination they had faced. But Ted never forgot. He began drawing cartoons for the school newspaper. The drawings combined his love of wordplay and fantastic creatures with his opinions about injustice and inequality.

To protect his true identity, Ted signed his cartoons "T. S. LeSieg" (LeSieg was Geisel spelled backward). In time, he would adopt the more famous pen name— Dr. Seuss—by which we know him today.

In 1921, Ted left Springfield to attend Dartmouth College in New Hampshire. Even though he was on his way to becoming an adult, memories of his hometown and the people there continued to influence his writing and his art. In fact, characters and places recalling those he knew from Springfield appear in Ted's first book, *And to Think That I Saw It on Mulberry Street*, and animals inspired by the zoo that he used to visit populate the stories of *Horton Hears a Who*. Two of his most famous characters, the Grinch and the Cat in the Hat, were based on the person Ted knew best of all— himself!

No matter how fanciful his stories became, to Ted they seemed as familiar as the Springfield town square or the shop around the corner. "Why write about Never-Never Lands that you've never seen," he once said, "when all around you have a real Never-Never Land that you know about and understand?"

A strong sensitivity to social injustice remained an important part of Ted's work as Dr. Seuss. In such books as *The Sneetches* and *Yertle the Turtle*, Ted warned about the dangers of discrimination, using words that readers of all ages can understand. He wrote in a

special language that he had developed all by himself—
and shared a lesson he had learned firsthand—as a kid
growing up on Mulberry Street.

# JACKSON POLLOCK

Boy on
the Move

**S**ometimes the best art school is the place where you grow up. As a kid, Jackson Pollock never took any drawing classes, never set foot in a museum, and never showed an interest in painting. Yet by the time he left the West for New York City at the age of eighteen, he had already learned more about art than any university could teach him.

**Some kids move around** a lot, but few live in as many places as Jackson Pollock did. By the time he was sixteen, he had lived in eight different cities in three states—from Wyoming to California to Arizona, then back to California (twice!), and once more to Arizona.

His family never stayed for long in any one place, but Jackson made the most of his boyhood tour of the western United States. At nearly every stop, he learned something that helped make him one of the world's most recognizable artists.

### FIRST STOP: CODY, WYOMING

Jackson was born in 1912 in this town named for its founder, Buffalo Bill Cody, the great Wild West show-man. Though he spent only the first ten months of his life there, Jackson never stopped reminding people that Cody was his hometown. That's how important the lore of the Old West was to him. In fact, when Jackson moved to New York City to become an artist, he was known for strutting around town in a cowboy hat and boots. Some people laughed at his rodeo garb, but Jackson was just being true to his heritage.

## AGES ONE TO FIVE: PHOENIX, ARIZONA

After a brief time in San Diego, California, the Pollock family moved to Phoenix when Jackson was just a toddler. His parents purchased a small farm on the outskirts of the city. For the next four years, Roy and Stella Pollock raised hogs, cows, and chickens and sold eggs, melons, and apricots at the local market. It was in Phoenix that Jackson learned an important lesson: he was not cut out to be a farmer.

HE'S BEEN STARING AT THAT WALL FOR A LONG TIME.

HMMMMM...

Jackson had a hard time adjusting to life in the desert. His family's three-room adobe house was very small. From April through October, Jackson and his four older brothers had to drag their beds outside and sleep in the yard. Although the stars shone brightly, Jackson was terrified of the wild landscape beyond.

In the daytime, Jackson refused to venture past the kitchen door unless his mother accompanied him. The farthest he dared go was a neighbor's house, where he hosted tea parties and played with a little girl who lived nearby.

On the rare occasions when Jackson did step outside, it seemed as if catastrophe always followed. One day when he was four years old, he found an old log in the barnyard and decided to chop it in half with an axe. An older boy named Charles Porter offered to do the job for him, because Jackson was too young to be using such a sharp tool.

The boys placed the wood on a chopping block. "Tell me where you want it cut," Charles said. Then, as Jackson pointed to a spot, Charles raised the axe high and slammed it down—*kerrunk*—splitting the log and lopping off the tip of Jackson's right index finger.

Jackson ran screaming to his mother, who quickly bandanged the wound. To add insult to injury, an old bull rooster had ambled by and gobbled up his severed fingertip.

(Jackson's finger never fully healed. Whenever he was photographed, he always hid his right hand inside his pocket or behind his back.)

Yet another disaster befell Jackson when he was riding into town with his mother one day. An angry bull had escaped from its pen and charged at their wagon. The Pollocks' horse panicked, sending Jackson and his mother crashing to the ground.

Fortunately, a quick-thinking farmer happened to be passing by and was able to scoop them off the road to safety. The frightening incident stayed with Jackson throughout his life. Years later, he still had nightmares about the rampaging beast that had nearly trampled him.

It wasn't only large animals that caused trouble for Jackson. He even had run-ins with little creatures, too. One time he was tasked with clearing his family's farm of gophers, a job that sounds harmless enough. But not for Jackson. He was in hot pursuit of one of the elusive critters when suddenly it turned and attacked, biting down hard on his hand.

"Take him off! Take him off!" Jackson wailed. His brother Charles swooped in and dislodged the furious gopher. Fortunately, Jackson escaped without losing another finger.

### AGES FIVE TO EIGHT: CHICO, CALIFORNIA

Jackson was not alone in his difficulty adapting to life in Arizona. His mother also wasn't happy there. So in 1917 she convinced her husband to auction off the family's livestock and move to Chico, California, where they purchased a small fruit farm.

Picking peaches off trees turned out to be a lot easier than milking cows and slopping hogs, and the Pollock boys had plenty of time for other pursuits.

Jackson's brother Charles was the first to become interested in art. A sensitive boy with a talent for calligraphy, Charles dazzled his family with lifelike drawings of pigs and submarines. At their mother's urging, he was excused from farm work and took weekly painting lessons at the home of an art tutor. Before long, Charles was spending most of his time in his room, mixing oil paints and clipping illustrations out of magazines to create a "library of art."

Not only did Charles love to make art, he also liked to cultivate the look of an artist. He grew his hair long, wore expensive silk shirts, and—using money he saved from his paper route—bought himself a pair of fancy shoes. Although Jackson showed no interest in drawing or painting, he began to envy the dapper, sophisticated image Charles was fashioning for himself. Now when people asked what he wanted to be when he grew up, Jackson replied: "I want to be an artist, like Charles."

The next stop for the Pollock family was Janesville, a town on the border between California and Nevada. Here, Jackson's parents tried something different: running a small hotel.

During the year he spent here, Jackson made friends with two Native American boys in his school. Orlo Shinn and Cecil Williams were known as the best illustrators in his class. They could draw horses bucking in just about every position. They knew rope tricks, too, which impressed Jackson even more.

Another encounter with Native Americans also left a lasting impression. One morning, Jackson was hiking with his brothers when a group of Wadatkut Indians passed by. The boys followed them to a clearing just outside town. From the shelter of pine trees, they watched as more than a hundred tribespeople gathered around a ceremonial pole. Suddenly a man wearing a bearskin appeared. With a blood-curdling shriek, he charged into the circle. Then he led the group in a ritual called a Bear Dance.

As the crowd began to chant, the "Bear" pulled people inside the circle to dance with him. Others poked the Bear with sticks. When the Pollock boys asked about the event, they learned that for the Wadatkut, dancing—as well as painting—was a sacred form of art that brought them closer to the spirits of their ancestors.

When Jackson grew older, this connection to the unseen spirit world would become a focal point of his own art-making.

In 1923, after three years in Janesville and the nearby town of Orland, California, Jackson and his family returned to Phoenix.

AAAAND WE'RE BACK!

By this time, much had changed. Jackson's brother Charles had left home to attend art school in Los Angeles. His father was supporting the family by working as a land surveyor for the United States government. And Jackson was no longer a kid scared of being chased by gophers. Yet although he had grown up while moving from place to place, Jackson still had another lesson to learn.

One day, Jackson and his brother Sande were hiking through ancient Native American ruins outside of Phoenix. The boys had often visited the site, exploring the cliff dwellings and hunting for arrowheads. But this time an altogether different surprise awaited them.

With their father leading the way, the boys scaled a high cliff wall and stood on the ledge overlooking Cherry Creek Canyon. There, on the back wall, they discovered a tiny doorway. It led to a secret room used by the ancient Indians who had carved the cliff out of the sheer rock face more than five centuries earlier.

Following the beam of their father's flashlight, the brothers gazed upon the wall. What they saw was a set of human handprints left behind by the masonry workers who had toiled inside the chamber hundreds of years before. As the boys took turns placing their own hands against the imprints, Jackson realized that this mark was the ancient Indian artisan's way of "signing" his work.

Years later, Jackson Pollock would sign his abstract "drip paintings" in the same way—with a carefully placed handprint, as if to say "Jackson was here." From Cody to Phoenix and all the places between, he had made the West his classroom. And everywhere he went, he learned something new.

# CHARLES SCHULZ

The Shy Guy

Long before he created Charlie Brown, Snoopy, and the rest of the Peanuts gang, Charles "Sparky" Schulz was just a quiet kid with a sketchpad who felt uncomfortable sharing his drawings with others. Only by overcoming his shyness could he make the leap from secret doodler to superstar cartoonist.

**Charles Schulz's father,** Carl, loved comics. In the 1930s he owned a thriving three-chair barbershop in St. Paul, Minnesota. Every Sunday, Carl would buy four newspapers just so he could follow the adventures of Buck Rogers, Little Orphan Annie, and other cartoon characters who populated the "funny pages."

Charles, Carl's only child, came to share his father's passion for the newspaper comic strips. As a young boy, Charles was called "Sparky," named after a rickety race-horse in the comic strip "Barney Google." On weekdays, Sparky helped his dad in the barbershop. On weekends, he would head over to the office of the town newspaper. He'd press his nose against the glass windows and watch the weekly funnies roll off the presses.

WWHIRRRRRRR

Sparky soon learned that he could do more than just read the comics. He could draw them. At the end of a long day spent cutting and sweeping hair, Sparky and his father rode home together on the streetcar. On cold winter evenings—and Minnesota had many of those—Sparky would sketch scenes from their day, using his finger to draw in the steam-fogged window.

Sensing that their son had a knack for illustration, Sparky's parents gave him a small chalkboard to carry around. Sparky spent hours drawing pictures onto its dark surface. When he grew older, he moved on to sketchpads. He always kept a sharpened pencil in his pocket, in case the urge to doodle should strike. On more than one occasion, the pencil point poked a hole in his trousers.

HEY, YOU DROPPED YOUR PENCIL!

At first, Sparky kept his drawings private. He was shy and didn't like to call attention to himself. At family gatherings, he sat alone with his face buried in his sketchpad. He rarely joined in conversations with his relatives, but sometimes an aunt or uncle would ask what he was drawing. "Let him alone!" Sparky's mother would admonish them.

One time, Sparky's parents took him to visit his Aunt Clara in the Wisconsin countryside. Clara's son Reuben also liked to draw. In fact, Reuben impressed the adults with his drawing of a man sitting on a log. Sparky took one look at his cousin's sketch and thought, "I could do better than that!"

When Sparky was in kindergarten, his teacher handed out crayons and asked the class to draw something they had seen. Inspired by the harsh Minnesota winter, Sparky drew a man shoveling snow.

Then he added his own flourish: a leafy palm, a tree he had learned about from his Uncle Monroe, who lived in California. A less open-minded teacher might have criticized Sparky for letting his imagination run wild. Instead she praised his originality, saying, "Charles, you're going to be an artist someday!" After receiving such praise and encouragement, Sparky was a little less reluctant to share his art with other people.

Then one day, Sparky's friend Raymond showed off the cover of his looseleaf binder. On it he had drawn a man riding a bucking bronco. Sparky had never thought to display his drawings like that. Soon his own binder was festooned with sketches of cartoon characters like Mickey Mouse and Popeye. When his classmates noticed, they asked him to decorate their notebooks as well. Sparky was elated.

A newly confident Sparky began to excel at school. His grades soared, and he was allowed to skip the fourth grade. That seemed like a good idea at first, but it wound up being a terrible setback on the road to overcoming his shyness.

That's because Sparky was now the smallest kid in his class. He longed to be selected for the school Safety Patrol, but was turned down because he was too short.

Not only that, but the older kids weren't as impressed by his artwork as his younger classmates had been. When he was singled out for an award in penmanship, he could hear the other students snickering behind his back as he got up from his desk to receive his pin and certificate.

Once again, Sparky retreated into his bashful shell.

He rarely spoke in class and tried to hide his drawing ability. His grades began to suffer, and he was forced to repeat the eighth grade.

In junior high, Sparky even lost confidence in the one thing he knew he was good at. When assigned to write about William Shakespeare for English class, he came up with the idea to illustrate the paper with his own drawings. But then he decided against it. To his dismay, another boy followed through on a similar project and received high praise.

But inspiration was not far away. It took the form of a mischievous black-and-white beagle who convinced Sparky to believe in himself again. No, not Snoopy, although Sparky would one day base his famous creation on his childhood pet. This dog was called

Spike. And he was known to eat anything he could get his paws on.

Spike once scarfed down an entire rubber ball. Another time, he jumped onto Carl Schulz's dresser and gobbled up a wad of money from the barbershop. The pooch appeared to be indestructible—no matter what Spike ate, it just seemed to pass right through without causing him any problems.

One winter night, when Sparky was fourteen, he decided to use Spike's misbehavior as the inspiration for a cartoon. He drew a picture of the gluttonous beagle sitting up and added the caption: "A hunting dog that eats pins, tacks, and razor blades is owned by C. F. Schulz, St. Paul, Minn."

He signed his cartoon "Drawn by 'Sparky.'" Then

he did something unusual for such a shy boy. Instead of hiding the drawing in his sketchbook, he sent it to the editors of the "Ripley's Believe It or Not" comic strip. To Sparky's surprise, they agreed to publish it. On February 22, 1937, Sparky's drawing appeared in more than 300 newspapers worldwide.

Sparky was immensely proud of his achievement. Although he remained shy and suffered many setbacks as an artist—including when his high school yearbook committee rejected his drawings—he never again lost faith in his artistic abilities. And eventually others saw his skill, too. As a young man, he applied for a place in a correspondence course at the Federal School of Applied Cartooning in Minneapolis. His work was so good that the school offered him a position as an instructor.

The job was perfect for Sparky. The quiet introvert

who had disliked showing his art to others was now encouraging students to share their illustrations with him. Even better, Sparky had more time to work on his cartoons, including one about a group of kids and a pet dog. His creation—"Peanuts"—became the world's most popular comic strip. Its main character, Charlie Brown, was just like Sparky: a boy filled with self-doubt who takes inspiration from his brash, mischievous beagle.

Charlie Brown may never have received the recognition he deserved, but Charles Schulz certainly did. He was rewarded with the admiration of millions of comics fans worldwide.

# YOKO ONO

Reversal of Fortune

**A**s an adult, Yoko Ono made the pursuit of peace an important part of her work as an activist and an artist. But back when she was a child, she got a firsthand look at how war can change a family when her comfortable life was upended by the outbreak of conflict between the United States and Japan.

**On a snowy February** night in 1933, Eisuke and Isoko Ono welcomed their first child into the world. They called her Yoko, meaning "Ocean Child." It was a fitting name for a girl who would one day sail across the ocean waters separating her native Japan from her adopted home in the United States.

Yoko Ono was born into a wealthy and powerful family. Her mother was the daughter of a prominent nobleman. Her father was a prosperous banker descended from a line of samurai warriors and a ninth-century Japanese emperor.

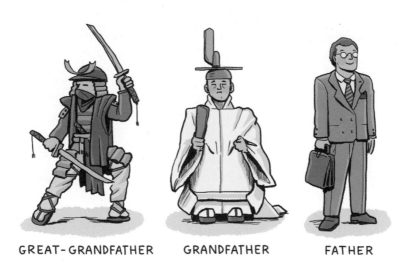

GREAT-GRANDFATHER      GRANDFATHER      FATHER

As a child, Yoko had thirty servants. Her mother preferred to live a life of leisure, and her father was often away on business. Yoko was looked after by maids, nannies, and private tutors. It was a stifling atmosphere. The servants lived in fear of being fired. They were instructed to enter and leave Yoko's room on their knees and to cater to her every whim. Whenever she traveled by train, attendants carrying cotton balls and rubbing alcohol followed after her. Their job was to disinfect any surface that Yoko might sit on.

Yoko didn't ask—or want—to be treated this way. Because of her social status, she often felt isolated and alone. She had few friends, and so she would try to play with the servants' children. But that was no fun. They were afraid of doing something wrong that would get their parents in trouble. At dinnertime, Yoko ate alone as a servant watched over her in silence.

But sometimes the domestic workers would try to entertain Yoko. One time, a servant wanted to teach Yoko traditional Japanese children's songs. But when Yoko's mother found out, she was horrified. She considered such "peasant music" too coarse and common for a girl of regal background.

I REFUSE TO LET YOU HEAR ANY MORE "PEASANT" MUSIC.

Isoko Ono resolved to send her daughter to the most exclusive private school she could find. So when Yoko was four years old, her mother enrolled her in Jiyu Gakuen, one of the most prestigious girls' schools in Japan. It was famous for its music program.

At Jiyu Gakuen, Yoko was exposed to the arts for the first time. She began taking piano and singing lessons. For one homework assignment, Yoko was told to memorize the noises she heard on the street, like a bird singing or a car horn honking, and then translate the sounds into musical notes. At the end of the semester, Yoko gave her first piano recital. She was so nervous that, as soon as the concert was over, she ran offstage and threw up.

At the end of the academic year, Yoko's mother decided that Jiyu Gakuen wasn't good enough. She transferred Yoko to an even more private school named Gakushuin. There Yoko continued her music studies. She also started drawing and writing haiku, an ancient form of poetry made up of three lines that contained precisely seventeen syllables.

Yoko's mother also began to teach Yoko how to paint. Sometimes Isoko Ono's instruction could be overbearing. For example, she had a habit of completing her daughter's assignments for her. One day Yoko was asked to show one of her paintings to the class. But it was mostly her mother's work. When everyone complimented the painting, Yoko felt embarrassed, instead of feeling proud. She couldn't accept praise she did not deserve.

YOU'RE DOING A GREAT JOB, HONEY.

In 1940, when Yoko was seven, her family moved to the United States. Her father had been transferred to a new job at a bank in New York City. Yoko began learning about American customs and fashions. But the move was not permanant. Soon Eisuke Ono was transferred again, and the family returned to Japan.

Only a year had passed, but much had changed in Tokyo, the Japanese capital. There were rumblings of a war between Japan and the United States, which caused problems for Yoko. She had taken on some new habits from her time in New York and had begun wearing American-style skirts and blouses. Some of the school-children taunted her. They called her an American spy and demanded that she wear traditional Japanese clothing. But Yoko refused to be bullied.

On December 7, 1941, World War II began when Japanese bombers attacked the American fleet at Pearl Harbor, in Hawaii. At first, the Ono family's wealth shielded them from many hardships. Yoko's parents had to release a few servants, allowing them to work in hospitals and factories. The Japanese government also made Yoko's mother turn over her diamond jewelry to help pay for the war effort. But otherwise, life went on as usual. The Onos could afford to have an underground bomb shelter, equipped with food and water in casc of emergencies.

As the conflict dragged on, however, the family's life began to change. Tokyo was bombed ferociously by American planes, and air raids were more frequent. The

Onos were often rousted out of bed at night and sent rushing to hide in their underground bunker. When it was safe again, Yoko would crawl out and watch as fires consumed the houses all around her.

Yoko's mother worried about her daughter. She decided to take Yoko out of school and move south, to a small farming village far from the heavy bombing. Almost overnight, the Onos went from a grand home full of servants to a tiny farmhouse in a cornfield. The building had no roof, but it was the best they could do.

Life in the village was hard. Because of wartime shortages, Yoko and her family had to depend on their neighbors for food. But the local farmers had trouble feeling generous. They wondered, Who are these wealthy city people demanding our meager rations?

The Onos were forced to beg for food while pulling around all their possessions in a wheelbarrow.

They also traded expensive jewelry and other items for basic necessities. Her mother bartered a treasured sewing machine for a large sack of rice to feed the family.

Yoko began going to school, but again she was bullied because of her family's wealth. Sometimes farm boys would throw rocks at her, but Yoko refused to back down. When other children called her names, she shouted back at them. With few friends to help during this difficult time, Yoko began to concentrate on poetry and art. "Art allowed me to communicate in a way that didn't require so much courage," she later said.

The war took its toll on the Onos, but Yoko's mother encouraged her daughter to remember everything she was witnessing. "You can write about this one day when it's over," she said. Just the thought that someday the fighting would end comforted Yoko. Thinking about how she could transform her experience into art, she instantly felt better.

In August of 1945, World War II ended with as much horror as it began: the United States dropped atomic bombs on two Japanese cities, killing many people. After surrendering, Japan began a long period of rebuilding. Yoko returned to Tokyo and her old school at Gakushuin. One of her new classmates was Prince Akihito, the son of Japan's emperor and the country's future ruler.

Yoko's days of begging for food and dodging bombs were over, but she did not return to her old pampered life. Like many survivors of war, she was a different person now. She decided she wanted to be a poet when she grew up. Over time, Yoko would learn to blend words and ideas with images, a style that would come to be called Conceptual Art. Her performances and music became known throughout Japan and, later, in England and America. Her marriage to the musician John Lennon in the 1960s brought her even more fame.

There was another important consequence of Yoko Ono's reversal of fortune—one whose effects are still felt today. Her wartime experience had left her with a strong distaste for conflict. Pacifism, or the belief that disputes should be settled nonviolently, became an important theme in her art, music, and writing. Her call for peace has inspired many other people to take up the cause, too.

# JEAN-MICHEL BASQUIAT

## The Anatomy Lesson

They called him the "Radiant Child," a teenage sensation whose colorful graffiti-style paintings made him one of the most celebrated artists of the 1980s. But before he upended the art world, Jean-Michel Basquiat found inspiration in the dusty pages of an old medical textbook.

In less than a decade, Jean-Michel Basquiat went from sleeping on the streets of New York City to hanging his paintings in its priciest art galleries. Even though he had no formal training, the Brooklyn native revolutionized the art world with his big, bold, graffiti-inspired artwork.

Basquiat's journey from teenage graffiti artist to international superstar began in a cramped crawl space under the stairs of the four-story Brooklyn brownstone where he lived with his parents and two younger sisters. The crawl space served as Jean-Michel's bedroom.

There was a mattress on the floor—and in fact, the mattress *was* the floor—and a comic-book-style drawing on the surface of every wall. This was Jean-Michel's fortress of solitude, and his first studio.

Jean-Michel began drawing at the age of three, using paper that his father, Gerard, brought home from the accounting firm where he worked. Jean-Michel's earliest subjects were television cartoon characters from the 1960s, like Fred Flintstone and Bullwinkle. His first art teacher was his mother, Matilde, who had a keen eye for color and had once worked as a clothing designer. She spent many hours drawing with her son, showing Jean-Michel how to copy scenes from the family Bible onto paper napkins.

"THE CONVERSION OF ST. PAUL." CRAYON ON NAPKIN.

When Jean-Michel was a little older, Matilde took him to the great art museums of New York City, like the Museum of Modern Art and the Metropolitan Museum of Art. By age six, Jean-Michel was already enrolled as a junior member of the Brooklyn Museum of Art. He even had a favorite painting: *Guernica* by Pablo

Picasso. He could also speak three languages: English, Spanish, and French. He was a renaissance kid.

Jean-Michel decided early on that he wanted to be a cartoonist when he grew up. At school, he spent most of his time doodling in a notebook. The other kids knew he was the class artist because he always walked around with several pencils sticking out of his hair.

When he was only seven, Jean-Michel completed his own children's book with his friend Mark Prozzo. He also created a comic strip with ten characters, including a mad scientist named Mr. Oopick. Not only that, but he drew ace caricatures of famous people, including the movie director Alfred Hitchcock and Alfred E. Neumann, the gap-toothed mascot of *Mad* magazine.

He mailed one of his drawings to J. Edgar Hoover, the director of the FBI in Washington D.C., hoping perhaps for recognition from the federal government. Hoover never replied.

Yet as devoted as he was to his craft, Jean-Michel was far from the best artist in his class. His drawings were often sloppy and needlessly abstract. He never won any painting contests. "I remember losing to a guy who did a perfect Spider-Man," he recalled. Though he yearned to be the best, he had not yet found the best way to express himself.

Sometimes it takes many years for an artist to develop a unique style. Other times, inspiration hits all at once. In Jean-Michel's case, it happened literally by accident. One day shortly after his seventh birthday, Jean-Michel was playing ball in the street when a car careened out of control and struck him. He was rushed to the hospital, where doctors diagnosed him with a broken arm and serious internal injuries. A surgeon determined that Jean-Michel's spleen had to be removed—and fast.

The surgery went smoothly, but Jean-Michel spent the next month recovering in his hospital bed. To keep him occupied, Jean-Michel's mother gave him a copy of a classic medical textbook called *Gray's Anatomy*. The book was filled with detailed drawings of the inner workings of the human body, and it fascinated Jean-Michel. He studied it day and night, memorizing the names of the various bones and body parts depicted

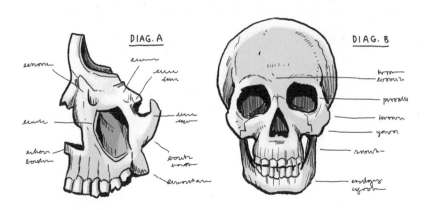

in the pages: the tibia, the femur, the aorta, and so on.

When he left the hospital, Jean-Michel brought the book home. It would remain with him always, a permanent reference he turned to again and again as he moved beyond cartoon drawings toward bolder, more sophisticated renderings of the human form.

In fact, many of Jean-Michel's paintings display what's been called his "X-ray vision" effect. They depict skeletons and skulls, covered with words, letters, and diagrams, just like the illustrations in *Gray's Anatomy*. Jean-Michel was so excited by his favorite book that he even formed a rock band named Gray, in its honor.

Jean-Michel had found a source of inspiration, but it would take time before he could harness his creativity to make art. The rest of his childhood was tumultuous and unhappy. Soon after he went home from the hospital, his parents decided to separate. Left in the custody of his father, who paid little attention to him, Jean-Michel grew increasingly angry and began to act out at home and at school. His grades suffered, and he was the only student to fail ninth-grade life-drawing class.

Increasingly isolated from friends and family, Jean-Michel ran away several times. He pulled pranks and got in trouble. He was even expelled from high school for dumping a box of shaving cream on the principal's head during the graduation ceremony.

By the age of seventeen, Jean-Michel was homeless, earning a meager living selling T-shirts and handmade postcards. His only means of expressing himself was by spray-painting graffiti on the sides of abandoned buildings. In an era when street art was just coming into fashion, that activity proved to be Jean-Michel's ticket to success.

In 1980, Jean-Michel met Andy Warhol, the Pop Art pioneer. Andy shared Jean-Michel's childlike view of the world and helped expose his new friend's work to museums and art collectors. Soon people were paying top dollar to display Jean-Michel's graffiti artworks in their galleries. Some even asked him to decorate their homes. Jean-Michel traveled all over Europe and around the United States on special commissions from wealthy art patrons. He became one of the most recognizable artists of the 1980s.

It took only a few years for Jean-Michel to go from spraying his "tag" all over lower Manhattan to selling his paintings for millions of dollars and changing the face of contemporary art. When he died in 1988 at the age of twenty-seven, the name that he had once spray-painted on walls was known all over the world.

# THREE

## PRACTICE MAKES PERFECT

IF YOU WANT TO BE A **SUCCESSFUL ARTIST,** YOU'LL NEED TO PAINT A LOT OF CANVASES. FORTUNATELY, EACH OF

——— THESE ———

# KID ARTISTS

HAD A TEACHER OR FRIEND CHEERING FOR THEM TO SUCCEED.

# CLAUDE MONET

## Impress to Success

You're never too young to make a good first impression. In just a few short years, Claude Monet went from selling humorous drawings on the streets of his hometown to helping invent his own style of painting. And he owed it all to the kindly stranger who convinced him to put down his pencil and pick up a paintbrush.

Claude Monet disliked being cooped up inside. Growing up in the French port city of Le Havre, he would often skip school to roam the beaches along the Normandy coast. Or he would wander the docks, listening to the workers speak in foreign languages as they unloaded cargo ships. The outdoors felt like his natural habitat.

"School was always like a prison to me," Claude later recalled. "I could never bring myself to stay there when the sun was shining and the sea was so tempting, and it was such fun scrambling over cliffs and paddling in the shallows."

Claude inherited his love of nature from his mother, Louise-Justine Aubrée Monet, a refined and elegant woman who liked to paint and write poetry. She used to carry around a pocket-sized sketchbook all the time, the better to record her impressions of the town and its inhabitants.

By contrast, Claude's father spent most of his time indoors. Claude-Adolphe Monet was a grocer by trade. He preferred that his second son follow him into the family business, but Claude didn't want that job. From an early age, he set his sights on becoming an artist.

CLAUDE, ARE YOU DONE STOCKING THE FRUIT?

At school, Claude was drilled in Latin and Greek, reading and arithmetic. He also took an art class with a French painter named François-Charles Ochard, who tried to teach him how to draw figures in the classical style. But Claude was far too independent-minded to follow Ochard's instruction. "I was born undisciplined," he later said. "Never, even as a child, could I be made to obey a set rule. What little I know I learned at home."

Instead of copying figures out of textbooks, Claude liked to doodle in the margins. He filled page after page with sketches of sailing ships and funny portraits of his teachers. "I drew the faces and profiles of my schoolmasters as outrageously as I could," he said, "distorting them out of all recognition." At family picnics, Claude would hand out sketchbooks to relatives and challenge them to a drawing contest. He always won.

A family friend named Théophile Beguin-Billecocq encouraged Claude by buying some of his pictures. "His sketches, whether in crayon or pencil, were always excellent," Billecocq wrote in his journal. "He knew how to capture the essential characteristics of a scene."

Before long, Claude became well known in his town for his amusing caricature sketches. Passersby would ask him to draw their picture and pay him ten francs a sketch. Within a month, the young artist's clientele had doubled—and so had his fee. "Had I gone on like that I'd be a millionaire today," he later said.

The owner of the local art supply store started hanging Claude's pictures in his shop window. Each week, a new one would appear. Soon there were five or six of Claude's caricatures lined up in a row, each one in its own golden frame, like a work of fine art. Claude swelled with pride every time one of his neighbors walked by and recognized the person portrayed in his pictures.

One day the shop owner introduced Claude to a man who would change his life forever. Eugène Boudin was a local landscape painter who liked to work outdoors, or en plein air, as the French would say. Boudin liked to paint beach scenes and images of ships moored in the harbor. He had seen some of Claude's drawings and thought he had potential to be a painter, too.

"I always look at your sketches with much pleasure," Boudin told him. "They are amusing, clever, and bright. You are gifted. One can see that at a glance. But I hope you are not going to stop at that. It is all very well for a beginning, but soon you will have enough of caricaturing."

Boudin invited Claude to paint with him in the open air. "Study, learn to see and to paint, draw, make landscapes. They are so beautiful, the sea and the sky, the animals, the people and the trees, just as nature has made them, with their character, their true existence in the light and the air, just as they really are."

At first, Claude declined Boudin's invitation. Though he loved the outdoors, he had never painted nature scenes. Besides, his caricatures already sold for far more money than Boudin's landscapes ever did.

YOU MUST COME WITH ME
AND PAINT THE OUTDOORS!

290, 295, 300...

Over the next several months, Boudin repeated his offer, but Claude always came up with a reason not to accompany him on his jaunts in the countryside. Finally, summer came, and with it the end of the school year. Claude had plenty of free time and had officially run out of excuses not to join Boudin. Besides, the weather was so nice that the idea of spending some time outside was starting to appeal to him.

So one day Claude gave in and went on an outdoor painting excursion with Boudin. Together they headed out to the coast, near the mouth of the Seine River.

Claude watched with fascination as Boudin daubed his canvas and began to paint the things he saw: the sandy beach, the open sky, the puffy clouds, the sunshine as it dappled the water. Looking on, Claude was overcome by a deep emotion. "I was enlightened," he said later. "It was as if a veil had been torn aside. I had grasped what painting could be."

Inspired by Boudin's example, Claude worked feverishly on his own canvas. It wasn't as good as Boudin's, but it was a start. Claude had found a new inspiration. "My way was clear, my destiny decreed," he said. "I would be a painter, come what may."

By this time, Claude was living with his aunt in Paris. While there he noticed many young painters copying the works of the old masters, just as he had done back in Monsieur Ochard's class. But thanks to his friend Boudin, Claude had found another path to making art. He spent his days standing by an open window painting what he saw.

Claude spent the next several years in Paris. He befriended many of the artists who would later join him in founding what became known as the Impressionist movement. Along with artists like Edouard Manet, Pierre-Auguste Renoir, and Paul Cézanne, Claude Monet went on to change the face of art forever. But he never forgot where it all began. If he had achieved any fame as an artist, he once admitted, "It is to Eugène Boudin that I owe the fact."

# PABLO PICASSO

> ## Problem Child
> ## Makes Good

"**E**very child is an artist," Pablo Picasso once observed. "The problem is how to remain an artist once we grow up." All his life, he chafed at the rules imposed on him by others. But what some people saw as a rebellious quality was in fact an imaginative and innovative spirit that could not be contained.

Pablo Picasso entered the world howling. Seconds after he was born, one of the hospital physicians, his uncle Don Salvador, leaned down and blew a huge cloud of cigar smoke in the newborn's face. The baby grimaced and bellowed in protest—and that's how everyone knew he was healthy and alive. At that time, doctors were allowed to smoke in delivery rooms, but this little infant would have none of it. Even at birth, he refused to accept things as they had always been done.

The baby was named Pablo Diego José Francisco de Paula Juan Nepomuceno María de los Remedios Cipriano de la Santísima Trinidad Martyr Patricio Clito Ruíz y Picasso—whew! He was known to his friends as Pablito, a nickname meaning "little Pablo," and he learned to draw before he could walk. His first word was *piz*, short for *lápiz*, the Spanish word for pencil. It was an instrument that would soon become his most prized possession.

Pablo inherited his love of art from his father, Don José Ruiz y Blasco, a talented painter. Don José's favorite subjects were the pigeons that flocked in the plaza outside the Picassos' home in Málaga, a town on the southern coast of Spain. Sometimes he would allow Pablo to finish paintings for him. One of Pablo's earliest solo artworks was a portrait of his little sister, which he painted with egg yolk.

But painting was not yet his specialty. Drawing was. Pablo mostly liked to draw spirals. When people asked him why, he explained that they reminded him of churros, the fried-dough pastries sold at every streetcorner stand in Málaga. While other kids played underneath trees in the Plaza de la Merced, Pablo stood by himself scratching circles in the dirt with a stick.

At school, Pablo found it hard to concentrate. Rather than completing classwork, he filled the margins of his notebook with pencil sketches of animals, birds, and people. His teacher grew exasperated with his lack of attention. She wrote a note to his mother saying: "Pablo should stop drawing in class and pay attention to his lessons."

It was clear that Pablo hated rules, and he took every opportunity to disobey them. When adults told him what to do, he did the opposite. He once got in trouble for coloring the sky a bright red instead of the "normal" blue. Pablo was often banished to the "calaboose," a bare cell with white walls and a bench, which served as a holding pen for unruly students.

"I liked it there, because I took along a sketch pad and drew incessantly," Pablo later said. "I could have stayed there forever drawing without stopping." He even began misbehaving on purpose so that he would be sentenced to detention and sent to the calaboose.

The one person who understood that Pablo wasn't acting out for no reason was his father. One day when Pablo's mother caught him drawing on the wall with a nail, Don José took him to the beach to blow off steam. As Don José stretched out to take a nap, Pablo sat beside him and drew a dolphin in the wet sand.

When Don José awoke, he was astonished by the beauty of his son's drawing. "Could it be Pablo who drew this?" he wondered.

That afternoon, Don José took a closer look at the image Pablo had drawn on their living room wall.

What at first looked like random scratches soon took shape. Don José recognized a reindeer and a bison running away from a group of men on horseback who were armed with bows and arrows. At that moment, Don José knew what to do to get Pablo to stop misbehaving. He decided to take him into his studio and teach his son how to paint.

From that day onward, Pablo and his father were inseparable art partners. In search of new subjects to portray, they began going to the bullfights. Pablo was mesmerized by the sight of the brave picadors as they charged ferocious bulls.

He saw El Lagartijo—"The Lizard"—one of the most famous bullfighters in Spain, and he met Cara Ancha, the celebrated Andalusian matador. When he was only nine years old, Pablo completed his first painting, *Le Picador*, a portrait of a man riding a horse in the bullring.

Two years later, Pablo's family moved to a new town, La Coruña, on Spain's Atlantic coast. Don José got a job as an art teacher at the local college. Even though he was much younger than the other students, Pablo enrolled in his father's class. He also took courses in figure drawing and landscape painting. By the time he turned thirteen, Pablo's skill level had surpassed his father's. Don José was so impressed that he handed his son his brushes and vowed never to paint again.

When Pablo was fourteen years old, his family moved again, this time to Barcelona, where Pablo enrolled in the prestigious School of Fine Arts. His teachers quickly noticed his skills and allowed him to skip two grades. But just as in Málaga, Pablo had trouble adhering to the school's rules. Before long he was back to his old tricks, cutting class so that he could wander the city streets, sketching interesting scenes that he observed along the way.

Pablo repeated this behavior at his next school, the Royal Academy of San Fernando in Madrid. This time, Pablo's father refused to tolerate his son's antics and stopped his allowance. At age sixteen, Pablo found himself on his own for the first time, forced to support himself on nothing but his artistic ability.

It has been said that the older Pablo grew, the more childlike his art became. During some periods he painted almost entirely in blue or depicted only circus performers. During his Cubist period, he painted people and objects broken down into geometric shapes. When he died in 1973, at the age of ninety-one, Pablo left behind more than fifty thousand artworks in a wide variety of styles and materials—paintings, prints, ceramics, sculpture, and more. He was considered the world's best-known artist.

When it came to making art, Pablo Picasso lived by his own rules. Wherever inspiration led him, he followed—something that would not have surprised anyone who had known him as a child growing up in his native Spain.

# FRIDA KAHLO

## Like Father, Like Daughter

**M**exico's most celebrated female artist, Frida Kahlo is known for her striking and sometimes shocking self-portraits and her distinctive personal style. As a girl growing up in Mexico, she found the strength to overcome adversity—and defy people's expectations—thanks in part to the positive example set by her father.

**Frida Kahlo and her** father had a lot in common. They both loved nature and the outdoors. They had the same dark eyes. They shared an interest in the art and archaeology of Mexico, the country they called home. But one thing above all else bonded them together: each had triumphed over a serious childhood illness.

Guillermo Kahlo had immigrated to Mexico from Germany as a young man. When he was boy, he had suffered an accident that damaged his brain, leaving him prone to epileptic seizures for the rest of his life. When she was growing up, Frida witnessed the aftermath of many of those seizures. Typically, they took place at night, just as Frida was going to bed. While her mother attended to Guillermo, Frida would lie awake wondering if her father would be okay. In the morning, he would be at the breakfast table, looking fit as a fiddle and acting as if nothing had happened.

GOOD MORNING, SUNSHINE!

Despite his condition, Guillermo became one of the most successful photographers in Mexico City. Frida often accompanied her father on his photography assignments. He taught her how to use a camera, how to develop photographs, and how to retouch pictures. Later, when Frida became a successful artist, she liked to pose the subjects of her paintings as if they were sitting in front of a camera.

Sometimes, in the middle of a shoot, Frida's father would be gripped by a seizure. He would suddenly fall to the ground and start convulsing. Luckily, Frida had learned what to do in these situations. She placed a cloth soaked in an anesthetic over his mouth and made him breathe into it until the seizure passed. In the meantime, she would watch over his equipment so that no one could steal it. After a few minutes, her father would recover and be back on his feet.

When Frida was six, she developed a serious medical condition. It began one day when she felt a horrible pain shooting down her right leg. A doctor diagnosed her with polio, a disease that causes the muscles in a person's legs to atrophy, or waste away. Today polio can be prevented with a vaccine, but in those days, there was no cure.

Frida spent the next nine months in bed; her doctors feared she might never walk again. But there was one person who knew better, one person who understood what it was like to live with a disability and not give up.

When Frida finally got out of her sickbed, she limped badly. Her right leg and foot had withered because of the disease. But Guillermo Kahlo had hope. He began nagging Frida to take up sports, something that was frowned upon for girls in Mexico at that time.

Inspired by her father's example, Frida began an epic athletic regimen. She played soccer, boxed, skated, took up wrestling, and became a champion swimmer. She rode her bicycle, climbed trees, and rowed a boat on the lakes of Chapultepec Park in Mexico City. Everywhere Frida went, her father was right by her side encouraging and helping her exercise.

But Guillermo did not stop there. He had a plan to exercise Frida's brain as well as her muscles. He gave her books from his own library. He took her down by the river to collect stones, insects, and unusual plants, which they brought home and examined together under a microscope. Most important, he presented his daughter with her first set of paints. Then, on Sundays, father and daughter would head out to the park to create watercolors together.

Frida emerged from her recovery period stronger both mentally and physically. But she would never be the same as before. Despite all her efforts, her right leg remained much thinner than the left. To disguise her disability, she began wearing boys' pants. Sometimes she put on three or four socks over her right calf. To balance out her uneven height, she wore a shoe with an extra-high heel.

While most of Frida's friends admired her dedication to persevering through her illness, some children made fun of her. At school, they called her "Frida, *pata de palo*" (Frida peg leg). Others singled her out for her tomboyish clothes. Sometimes when she went whizzing by on her bike, one of the other kids' mothers would shout in Spanish, "What an ugly girl!"

But Frida never let her injured leg keep her from

doing what she wanted. "Feet?" she'd respond to anyone who teased her. "Why do I need them if I have wings to fly?" Just like her father, she had come to understand the importance of pressing on no matter what obstacles were placed in her path.

Frida had many more barriers to overcome before she became a world-renowned artist. When she was eighteen, she was in a terrible bus accident that left her with several broken bones. She spent three months in the hospital. During her convalescence, she began making the self-portraits for which she would one day be known worldwide.

"I paint myself because I am so often alone and because I am the subject I know best," she said later in life. All told, Frida would paint more than fifty such images, as well as numerous portraits of friends and family members.

Guillermo Kahlo died of a heart attack in 1941, when Frida was thirty-four years old and already finding success as an artist. After his death, Frida wrote in her diary: "My childhood was marvelous because, although my father was a sick man, he was an immense example to me of tenderness, of work and, above all, of understanding for my problems."

Shortly before she died, Frida painted one final portrait of her father. The inscription below the image reads: "I painted my father...artist-photographer by profession, in character generous, intelligent and fine, valiant because he suffered for sixty years with epilepsy, but he never stopped working." She signed the painting "With adoration, his daughter, Frida Kahlo."

# JACOB LAWRENCE

Little Kid,
Great Migration

Jacob Lawrence never forgot where he came from. A child of Harlem with roots in the South, this pioneering African American artist chronicled the "Great Migration" of his people during the first half of the twentieth century. His own journey began just a few blocks from home, in the local community center where he taught himself to create art using whatever materials he could find.

Birds migrate by flying south for the winter. The migration of Jacob Lawrence's family took them in the opposite direction. In the early 1900s, his parents left the rural South for Atlantic City, New Jersey, where Jake was born. After his parents separated when he was seven years old, Jake moved with his mother to a new home in Philadelphia, Pennsylvania.

But Jake wasn't the only new kid in town. In fact, a steady stream of people were arriving in the north after leaving their homes in the southern United States. Every few weeks, another family would move into the Lawrences' apartment building. Neighbors would donate their old clothes to help the new arrivals. Often these clothes were faded and patched, but the kids made the best of their hand-me-down wardrobes.

In 1930, when Jake was thirteen, he moved north again, this time to New York City, where his mother had found work as a cleaning woman. Jobs and houses were scarce in those lean economic times, especially for African Americans. Jake, his younger sister Geraldine, and his younger brother William squeezed into a cramped apartment in the densely populated neighborhood of Harlem.

Once again, Jake had to adjust to strange and unfamiliar surroundings: a new school and another set of friends. He missed the open space and the row houses he'd gotten used to in Philadelphia. Always a shy and solitary boy, he began to withdraw.

Jake's mother worried her son might fall in with the wrong crowd, maybe even join a gang, so she looked for afterschool activities to keep him occupied. One day she heard about a small community center called Utopia House that offered an arts and crafts program for kids every weekday afternoon. She knew Jake liked to draw, so she signed him up for classes.

On his first day at Utopia House, Jake met the art instructor, Charles Alston. "Can I color?" Jake asked, eyeing a bucket of crayons on a nearby table.

"Of course!" Mr. Alston replied. In fact, as Jake soon discovered, there was very little that was not permitted within the walls of Utopia House.

Charles Alston saw great potential in Jake. The boy's only limitation seemed to be a lack of art supplies. Before arriving at Utopia House, Jake never had access to the tools needed to express himself. His mother was unable to buy them. He did have a pad for doodling, and on Christmas he might get a set of paints as a present. But he never had the brushes, palettes, and pencils that a lot of young children take for granted.

But now he had everything he needed right at his fingertips. In the weeks that followed, Mr. Alston gave Jake clay to sculpt, soap to carve, reeds to make baskets, wood for woodwork, metal for metalwork, and crayons, pastels, and colored pencils for drawing.

Mr. Alston also gave Jake the most important art supply of all: encouragement. From the moment he watched Jake draw for the first time, he could see that the boy didn't need that much instruction. "I decided it would be a mistake to try to teach him," Mr. Alston said later. "He was teaching himself, finding his own way." Mr. Alston wouldn't even let Jake watch him as he painted, fearing that the boy would lose his way by trying to imitate his teacher.

At first, Jake drew simple colored shapes. When

he had trouble coming up with new ideas, Mr. Alston gave him some advice: "Look inside your own home for inspiration," he said. That night, Jake noticed that the decorations in his apartment had patterns, too. He studied the Persian rugs on the floor and the quilts his mother made. The next day at Utopia House, he drew those designs on his paper.

Over time, the patterns became more intricate. Jake even started to create his own original designs, using shapes and colors of his choosing. Sometimes he drew all blue triangles or all green rectangles. He was learning to let everyday objects spark his imagination.

Jake applied this same principle to his art projects at Utopia House. After seeing decorative masks in a magazine article about life in Africa, Jake wondered about a way to reproduce the same effect with the materials he had in Harlem. Jake asked Mr. Alston how to mix papier-mâché. Soon Jake was creating life-sized masks like the ones he had seen in the magazine.

One day, Jake decided that he wanted to paint a mural. No one would allow a kid to paint on a public wall, so Jake made his own wall out of an old cardboard box. He sliced off the top and then painted the remaining panels. With only a few simple tools, he created a three-dimensional street scene—the first of many he would complete over the next several years. Jake's cardboard murals depicted everyday life in the grocery stores, barbershops, and pool halls of Harlem.

"I didn't even realize it was art at the time," Jake said later of these early do-it-yourself projects. "I just did it because it was fun."

Just as Jake was starting to find his way as a young artist, the Great Depression struck and halted his education. His mother lost her job cleaning houses, and Jake had to set aside his art and focus on finding work to help support his family. Jake dropped out of school and spent several years working odd jobs. He collected junk and empty bottles off the streets, selling them for spare change. He dug ditches, delivered laundry, and worked in a printing plant.

Even though Jake no longer had time to make art, he continued to improve himself. He studied African American history. He learned all about the Great Migration, the mass movement of thousands of African Americans from the farms and towns of the South to northern cities. At last he understood that they had left their homes in search of better lives and jobs.

Eventually, Jake's mother went back to work, and Jake was able to resume his artistic education. He signed up for free classes at the Harlem Community Art Center, where he met another black artist named Augusta Savage. Augusta had once been a laundry worker, just like Jake, but now she was working as a sculptor. Augusta convinced Jake that he, too, could earn a living as an artist. She helped him get a job with the Works Progress Administration, a government agency that employed people to create public art.

Some of Jake's paintings during this period captured the hard times that had fallen on the people of Harlem during the economic depression. Others depicted scenes from the lives of African American historical figures whom Jake had read about, including the abolitionists Frederick Douglass and Harriet Tubman.

When Jake was twenty-three years old, he completed his most important artwork: the Migration Series. The series told the Great Migration story in sixty paintings, each on a separate cardboard panel. In some ways, this new work was not much different from the street scenes on boxes that Jake had created at Utopia House. Now he was working on an epic scale, blending words with images to relate the sweeping saga of the mass movement of people over many decades.

The Migration Series was a huge success. Jake's work was featured in national magazines, and he was hailed as one of America's up-and-coming artists. The journey that had begun when his parents left the South had come full circle. Jacob Lawrence had arrived.

# ANDY WARHOL

Mother
Knows
Best

**A**ndy Warhol's colorful portraits of famous people helped him become one of the most celebrated pop artists of the 1960s. But he might never have made it out of Pittsburgh if not for the love and support of the biggest superstar of them all—his mother, Julia.

Praised for his colorful portraits of cultural icons, Andy Warhol was known as the "Prince of Pop"—that is, Pop Art, a style of painting that he helped pioneer. However, the world he grew up in was anything but princely. In fact, Andy's parents often struggled to put food on the table for him and his two older brothers.

Andrei and Julia Warhola were immigrants who had moved to America from a small mountain village in the Carpathian Mountains of Eastern Europe, a region made famous by the author Bram Stoker in his horror novel *Dracula*. As an adult, Andy would be known to his friends as "Drella"—a combination of Dracula and Cinderella, two of his favorite fictional characters.

The Warholas settled in Pittsburgh, Pennsylvania, a city with a large immigrant community. Andrei,

Andy's father, worked in construction and was away from home a lot, seeking out odd jobs to make a living. Julia, Andy's mother, was the artist in the family. She was a whiz at crochet, loved to draw angels and cats, and carved flower sculptures out of old soup cans, which she sold to earn extra money for the household.

When Andy was born, his family lived in a cramped two-room apartment overlooking the Ohio River. The bathtub was in the middle of the kitchen. For a bathroom, they used an outhouse in an alley behind the building. At home, the Warholas spoke little English, communicating instead in a mixture of Ukrainian and Hungarian known as Po nasemu. The language barrier made it hard for Andy to talk to the other kids in his neighborhood. As a result, he became shy and had only a few close friends.

Andy had few luxuries when he was growing up, but he tried to make the best of what he had. His parents couldn't afford to buy him a bicycle, so he rode on the handlebars of his friend's bike. A dog was too expensive, so Andy kept a pet chicken—until one day his mother turned it into chicken soup. That was a feast compared

to the usual dinnertime fare in the frugal Warhola home: a bland "tomato soup" made from ketchup mixed with water, salt, and pepper.

When Andy was four years old, his older brother Paul enrolled him in the first grade at the local school. Andy was two years younger than most of his classmates, but Paul thought that being around other kids would cure him of his shyness. He was wrong. On the first day of school, a girl slapped Andy in the face. Andy was so upset that he cried all the way home and refused to go back the next day.

Paul thought Andy should return to class, but Andy's mother decided to let her son stay home until he was old enough to deal with strangers. For the next two years, while his brothers headed off to school, Andy remained behind with his mother. It turned out to be one of the happiest times of his life.

Andy's mother used their time together to teach her son about creating art. She shared her tin-can sculptures with him, and they took turns drawing pictures of the family cat.

When the weather was nice, she and Andy would go shopping downtown. One time, Andy's mother bought herself a black felt hat. Andy decorated it with gold paint around the edges. It was one of his first solo artistic creations.

Andy quickly developed a reputation as the local neighborhood's artist. When kids would play baseball in the street near his home, Andy positioned himself deep in the outfield—making it easy for him to scamper away when no one was looking. If the ball was hit in his direction, the other kids would discover that Andy was no longer there. He had run home to work on his illustrations. They found him sitting with his sketchbook, drawing flowers.

Andy's other interest was movies, and his hobby was to spend every Saturday morning at the neighborhood theater. His favorite film was *Alice in Wonderland* and his favorite actress was Shirley Temple. While his brothers toiled on their schoolwork, Andy read movie magazines and kept a scrapbook of photographs of

Hollywood stars. Eventually, he begged his mother to buy him a projector so he could watch movies at home.

Julia took a job doing housework until she'd saved up enough to buy the projector. She had no money left over for a screen, but Andy found a solution: he projected the cartoons onto the wall of his room. Then he drew copies of the characters in his sketchbook.

On Sundays, Andy and his mom attended religious services at the local Byzantine Catholic church. Within this quiet space, he became mesmerized by the rows of holy icons (paintings of saints) that hung over the altar. Later, when Andy became an artist, he modeled some of his portraits after these sacred images.

When Andy was six years old, it was decided that he would go back to school. He was still shy, but he was learning to get along with strangers. His favorite part of the school day was lunch, when he could go home and slurp down a bowl of Campbell's soup prepared by his mother.

Andy found that his drawing skills helped him impress the other kids. He drew portraits of his class-mates, decorated the blackboard with a special border according to the season, and created pictures for the classroom calendar. Teachers began to take notice of his artistic activities.

Just as Andy was starting to feel more comfortable in the classroom, he fell ill, stricken with a bad case of rheumatic fever. One of the complications of his illness was a condition called St. Vitus's Dance, a disorder that causes uncontrollable twitching. Andy now had trouble speaking clearly, his knees buckled when he walked, and he found it hard to tie his shoes or sign his name. When he tried to draw on the blackboard, his hand trembled. Some kids began to laugh at him. A few even started to push him around and bully him. Once again, Andy grew terrified of going to school.

On the advice of the family doctor, Andy was confined to his bed for a month. Andy's mother moved his bed into the dining room so she could watch over him. She gave him movie magazines, paper dolls, and comic books to keep him occupied.

Before long, Andy's hands stopped shaking and he started drawing again. He enthusiastically colored in his coloring books. Whenever he completed a page, his mother would reward him with a chocolate bar.

When Andy's prescribed month of bedrest was over, it was time to return to school. Andy insisted that he still felt sick, but no one but his mother believed him. His brother Paul insisted that he get back in the classroom, but Andy threw a tantrum and refused to budge. Since Andy's father was away at work, the Warholas' next-door neighbor came over, picked Andy up, and dragged him kicking and screaming to Holmes Elementary.

Almost immediately, Andy suffered a relapse and his symptoms returned. In fact, now they were even worse. In addition to shaking, he had pimples, blotchy skin, and a bulbous red nose. Kids called him "Spot" or "Andy the Red-Nosed Warhola."

Upset, Andy went back to bed for another month. He resumed drawing, and his condition steadily improved. This time, his family and friends knew better than to force him to return to school. The doctor informed them that Andy could suffer yet another relapse.

When Andy did go back to class, his older brothers looked out for him. They scared off bullies and warned away anyone who tried to make fun of him. They had come to understand that not only did Andy have a special talent, but he also required special care.

Slowly but surely, Andy began to improve at school, and his teacher suggested that he take free art classes at the nearby Carnegie Institute (now the Carnegie Museum of Art). Andy quickly became the star pupil and eventually developed the technical skills he would need to succeed as an artist.

But Andy was able to continue studying only because of his father's foresight back when he was still alive. Andy had lost his dad when he was thirteen years old. Andy was so upset that his father had died that he hid under his bed and refused to come out until the funeral was over. Fortunately for Andy and his future, Andrei Warhola had left plans to ensure that his son could fulfill his artistic potential.

That's because, unbeknownst to the family, Andrei had been saving money for Andy's education. Shortly before he died, Andrei took Andy's brother John aside and made him promise to look after his little brother. "You're going to be real proud of him," he said. "He's going to be highly educated."

In his will, Andrei directed that the money be spent on his youngest son's college education. And so in 1945, eighteen-year-old Andy enrolled at the Carnegie Institute of Technology to study pictorial design.

After graduation, he moved to New York City and worked as an illustrator. Shortly after that, Andy's mother left Pittsburgh and moved in with him.

Over the next twenty years, Andy became known

for his portraits and screenprints of ordinary household objects, like boxes of detergent and cans of soup. Throughout these years, his mother continued to cook, clean, and care for him just as she had when he was a boy. She also collaborated with Andy on art projects and published two books filled with drawings of cats.

Andy went on to become an international style icon known for his unique appearance. He often wore a white wig and dark sunglasses. And just like when he was a kid, his mother was always there for him, helping and inspiring him. She even became the subject of his art.

Andy established his mother's celebrity status for all time by painting her portrait. Today, the likeness of Julia Warhola hangs in the Andy Warhol Museum in Pittsburgh. Her portrait appears alongside his other glamorous portraits of stars from film, music, and pop culture, such as Marilyn Monroe, Elizabeth Taylor, and Elvis Presley. It is the ultimate homage to his number one fan.

# KEITH HARING

Through a Kid's Eyes

**W**hat if you could draw like a kid and become a well-known artist? Keith Haring did just that. His bold and colorful illustrations of crawling babies, dancing people, barking dogs, and rocking robots helped make him one of the most beloved artists of the 1980s.

"I can make any kid smile," Keith Haring once boasted. "It's probably from having a funny face and looking and acting like a kid. Kids can relate to my drawings, because of the simple lines."

One of Keith's most famous artistic creations was a vibrant, glowing infant known as the Radiant Baby. In the 1980s, Keith became famous for drawing this fun image on walls all over New York City.

For all we know, it might have been a self-portrait. Most babies are born facedown, but Keith entered the world beaming up at the ceiling—a position the doctor who delivered him called "sunnyside up." That happy glow quickly earned him the reputation as the cutest baby in his hometown of Kutztown, Pennsylvania. From the time he was very young, people on the street would stop what they were doing to say hello to him. Keith always said hello back.

When it came time to learn how to draw, Keith was just as eager to please. Every night after supper, he would sit on his father's lap, clutching crayons. Allen Haring, who made cartoons in his spare time, showed Keith how to make drawings out of connected circles. Sometimes Allen lined them up one after another to form a segmented worm. Or he put feet on the circles to create a dragon. By following his father's example, Keith learned to use a few simple strokes to turn a circle into a balloon or an ice cream cone or a face.

The more they drew, the more advanced the lessons became. Sometimes Keith's father would draw a line and tell Keith to draw another line. Then he would add a third line and so on. Back and forth they went until they had drawn an entire picture together. Keith's mother was in charge of stocking the house with art supplies. Once she made the mistake of thanking her son for not drawing on the walls. That gave Keith an idea.

One day when his dad was out painting the roof, Keith plunged his hands into an open paint can and pressed them against the cellar walls. "Look!" he said to his mother. "Now I've drawn on the walls!" That wouldn't be the last time Keith got into trouble for leaving his mark on a wall.

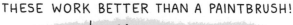

THESE WORK BETTER THAN A PAINTBRUSH!

It soon became clear that Keith had his own way of doing things. The usual activities bored him. He joined the Boy Scouts, but soon left the group. He briefly played Little League baseball, but he didn't really like sports, either. All his energy went into art, but even with that he was unconventional. When his father made him a drawing table out of an old sheet of plywood, Keith scribbled directly onto its surface rather than on paper. Soon the wood was covered in doodles.

As he grew older, Keith began spending more time alone in his room, making sketches and listening to music. He collected fan magazines devoted to pop groups like the Monkees and Herman's Hermits. Keith became so fascinated by the Monkees that he started cutting their photographs from the magazines and using them to make collages. He even started his own fan club, complete with a clubhouse that he constructed himself.

When he needed to escape from his parents' rules, Keith walked the five blocks to his grandmother's house. There, he was allowed to do all the things his parents forbade. On Saturday mornings, Keith would sit for hours watching cartoons of Walt Disney or Looney Tunes. The colorful characters on 1960s TV sitcoms also fascinated him. When Keith began painting as a professional artist, the bright colors and outrageous situations on these shows influenced his art.

Keith also liked to pore over his grandmother's copies of *Life* and *Look* magazines, searching for photographs he could turn into drawings. He flipped on the stereo and blasted songs by Iron Butterfly and the Rolling Stones. Inspired by the music, Keith began drawing scenes from classic fairy tales, which he populated with hippies.

As a teenager, Keith no longer drew as much with his father, but he still liked making art with others.

When his youngest sister, Kristen, showed an interest in art, they devised a fun activity: They would sit down facing each other, with a piece of paper on the table in front of them. They started drawing, and when Keith yelled "Stop!" they'd switch papers. Back and forth they went, until they completed their collaborative sketch.

Keith even showed Kristen how to paint with her hands—only this time he made sure to stay out of trouble with their mother. He smeared Kristen's hands with paint and then encouraged her to stamp them on paper (not the wall!). Soon the sheets were covered in colorful prints. Then they spent the rest of the afternoon cutting out the handprints and hanging them on a coat hanger to make a mobile.

Even when he was older, Keith never outgrew his mischievous streak, and he still liked to leave his mark on public spaces. When he was thirteen years old, Keith took a job delivering newspapers. One time, a customer was resurfacing the sidewalk in front of her house. Keith decided to carve his initials into the wet cement. Fortunately, the angry homeowner turned out to be the town's high school art teacher, Nita Dietrich.

Ms. Dietrich did not hold a grudge against Keith, especially after she saw his other artworks. In fact, she encouraged him to enter an upcoming art contest held in honor of America's bicentennial celebration in 1976.

Keith took up her offer. For his entry, he created a two-foot-tall map of the United States, with each state identified by a symbol. For instance, Florida was decorated with an image of Mickey Mouse. Keith's imaginative map won a prize—the first of many he would garner on his way to being an artist.

I'D LIKE TO THANK MRS. DIETRICH, MY SISTER, & ALL MY FRIENDS AT THE MONKEES CLUBHOUSE

After Keith graduated from high school, he studied commercial art at the Ivy School of Professional Art in Pittsburgh. He later moved to New York City, where he continued his education at the famed School of Visual Arts. It was there that Keith first began to make a name for himself as a street artist. He became friends with Jean-Michel Basquiat, another artist who shared his childlike view of the world as well as his fondness for drawing in public.

In the 1980s, Keith's graffiti-style drawings could be seen on the walls of subway stations all over New York City. Armed with pieces of white chalk, he turned the backgrounds of old ripped-out posters into his own personal canvas. Sometimes he would draw as many as forty pictures a day. Besides the Radiant Baby, Keith became known for drawing flying saucers, floating angels, and other colorful creatures from his imagination. As his drawings became popular, fans and admirers would cut them out out of their original street settings and hang them on their own walls.

Although his artworks became valuable collector's items, Keith was never in it for the money. After his death in 1990, a magazine published an article about him entitled "Kid Haring." It was the perfect way to remember an artist who never stopped seeing the world through a child's eyes.

I ACQUIRED THIS AT THE PRINCE STREET SUBWAY STATION

# FURTHER READING

WANT MORE
STORIES

— ABOUT THE —

KID ARTISTS

AND YOUR

FAVORITE
ARTWORKS?

TURN THE PAGE

AND KEEP
READING!

# BIBLIOGRAPHY

There are many great books about great artists, including autobiographies (books written by the person about himself or herself) and biographies (books about noteworthy people written by someone else). The following is a list of main sources used by the author in researching and writing this book.

## PART I

## CALL OF THE WILD

### Leonardo da Vinci

Giorgio Vasari, *The Lives of the Artists*. New York: Oxford University Press, 2008.

Liana Bortolon, *The Life and Times of Leonardo*. Philadelphia: Curtis Books, 1967.

Marco Rosci, *Leonardo*. New York: Mayflower Books, 1981.

Serge Bramly, *Leonardo: The Artist and the Man*. New York: Penguin Books, 1991.

# Vincent van Gogh

Jan Greenberg and Sandra Jordan, *Vincent Van Gogh: Portrait of an Artist.* New York: Dell Yearling, 2001.

# Beatrix Potter

Margaret Lane, *The Tale of Beatrix Potter.* New York: Penguin, 1986.

Sarah Fabiny, *Who Was Beatrix Potter?* New York: Grosset & Dunlap, 2015.

# Emily Carr

Emily Carr, *Growing Pains: The Autobiography of Emily Carr.* New York: Oxford University Press, 1946.

Maria Tippett, *Emily Carr: A Biography.* New York: Oxford University Press, 1979.

# Georgia O'Keeffe

Hunter Drohojowska-Philp, *Full Bloom: The Art and Life of Georgia O'Keeffe.* New York: W. W. Norton, 2004.

Jeffrey Hogrefe, *O'Keeffe: The Life of an American Legend.* New York: Bantam Books, 1992.

# PART TWO

## IT'S A HARD-KNOCK LIFE

## Louise Nevelson

Laurie Lisle, *Louise Nevelson: A Passionate Life*. New York: Simon & Schuster, 1990.

Natalie S. Bober, *Breaking Tradition: The Story of Louise Nevelson*. New York: Atheneum, 1984.

## Dr. Seuss

Donald E. Pease, *Theodor Seuss Geisel*. New York: Oxford University Press, 2010.

Judith Morgan and Neil Morgan, *Dr. Seuss & Mr. Geisel*. Boston: Da Capo Press, 1995.

## Jackson Pollock

Deborah Solomon, *Pollock: A Biography*. New York: Simon & Schuster, 1987.

Steven Naifeh and Gregory White Smith, *Pollock: An American Saga*. New York: Clarkson Potter, 1989.

## Charles Schulz

Beverly Gherman, *Sparky: The Life and Art of Charles Schulz*. San Francisco: Chronicle Books, 2010.

David Michaelis, *Schulz and Peanuts*. New York: Harper, 2008.

# Yoko Ono

Jerry Hopkins, *Yoko Ono*. New York: Macmillan, 1986.

Nell Beram and Carolyn Boriss-Krimsky. *Yoko Ono: Collector of Skies*. New York: Amulet Books, 2013.

# Jean-Michel Basquiat

Phoebe Hoban, *Basquiat: A Quick Killing in Art*. New York: Penguin, 1998.

# PART III

## PRACTICE MAKES PERFECT

# Claude Monet

Ann Waldron, *Who Was Claude Monet?* New York: Grosset & Dunlap, 2009.

Matthias Arnold, *Monet*. London: Haus Publishing, 2005.

# Pablo Picasso

Arianna Huffington, *Picasso: Creator and Destroyer*. New York: Avon Books, 1988.

John Richardson, *A Life of Picasso*. New York: Knopf, 1991.

True Kelley, *Who Was Pablo Picasso?* New York: Grosset & Dunlap, 2009.

# Frida Kahlo

Barbara C. Cruz, *Frida Kahlo: Portrait of a Mexican Painter.* Springfield, N.J.: Enslow, 1996.

Hayden Herrera, *Frida: A Biography of Frida Kahlo.* New York: HarperCollins, 1983.

# Jacob Lawrence

Peter D. Nesbett and Michelle DuBois, *Over the Line: The Art and Life of Jacob Lawrence.* Seattle: University of Washington Press, 2000.

Romare Bearden and Harry Henderson, *A History of African-American Artists: From 1792 to the Present.* New York: Pantheon, 1993.

# Andy Warhol

Tony Scherman and David Dalton, *Pop: The Genius of Andy Warhol.* New York: HarperCollins, 2009.

Victor Bockris, *Warhol: The Biography.* Boston: Da Capo Press, 2003.

# Keith Haring

John Gruen, *Keith Haring: The Authorized Biography.* Whitby, Ontario: Fireside Publishing, 1991.

# INDEX

## S

## T

## V

Vermeer, Jan, 29
victory gardens, 81

# ACKNOWLEDGMENTS

**DAVID STABLER** would like to thank Jason Rekulak, Mary Ellen Wilson, and the entire staff at Quirk Books. Special thanks to Nicole De Jackmo and Kelly Coyle-Crivelli for helping spread the word about the Kid Legends series. Kudos to Doogie Horner for another charmingly jocose set of illustrations.

**DOOGIE HORNER** would like to thank my wife, Jennie, as always for helping me make the time, space, and coffee necessary to draw this book. Thanks also to Jason Rekulak for originally proposing this series, David Stabler for writing it, Mario Zucca for coloring the illustrations, Mary Ellen Wilson for editing the words, and Andie Reid and Molly Murphy for designing the interior. Special thanks to Bill Thwing for letting me draw in his office, and to my parents for encouraging me when I was a kid artist myself. This book is dedicated to Kirby Horner.

# THEY'RE LITTLE KIDS WITH BIG DREAMS... AND BIG PROBLEMS!

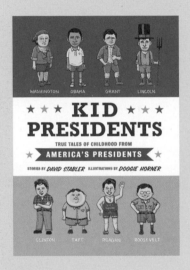

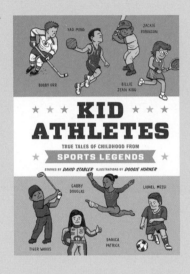

John F. Kennedy hated his big brother. Lyndon Johnson pulled pranks in class. And Bill Clinton was crazy clumsy (he once broke his leg jumping rope). Plus stories about George Washington, Abraham Lincoln, Barack Obama, Ronald Reagan, and more!

Babe Ruth was such a trouble-maker, his parents sent him to reform school. Race car champion Danica Patrick fended off bullies who told her "girls can't drive." And Peyton Manning was forced to dance the tango in his school play. Plus stories about Jackie Robinson, Michael Jordan, Lionel Messi, and more!

## READ ALL OF THE BOOKS IN THE KID LEGENDS SERIES.
### AVAILABLE EVERYWHERE BOOKS ARE SOLD.